"Jody Sokolower weaves a transnational story across settler-colonial geographies from Northern California to East Jerusalem to illuminate ongoing struggles for land and freedom. Using her personal story as a teacher in community with young people, she highlights the entwinements of knowledge and power that reinforce oppressive status quos and possible futures by forefronting the stories of Palestinian youth, who speak loudly and clearly in their own voices. *Determined to Stay* is a must-read book for all ages and stands to fill a critical gap in US standard curricula."

—**Noura Erakat, activist and human rights attorney, author of *Justice for Some: Law and the Question of Palestine*, co-editor of *Jadaliyya***

"What a treasure this book is. In story after story, *Determined to Stay: Palestinian Youth Fight for Their Village* invites young people—and all the rest of us—into the lives of Palestinians. We witness their struggles and the daily outrages that make life for young Palestinians so hard. Sokolower's book is a testament to resilience and people's remarkable tenacity in braiding lives of dignity. And it does not leave these issues 'over there.' An Indigenous activist in California tells Sokolower: 'To decolonize is to tell the truth.' Poignant and personal, *Determined to Stay* brings Palestine to life for US students."

—**Bill Bigelow, Curriculum Editor, Rethinking Schools, co-editor of *A Peoples Curriculum for the Earth***

"As a Palestinian high school educator and mother of school-aged children, *Determined to Stay* is the book I have been waiting for. This is the book I want my own children reading in their classrooms. It is one of the few contemporary books that sheds light on the current reality of Palestinians and is written particularly for middle and high school students, although it can be adapted for use with upper elementary grades. The history and current reality of the people of Silwan is reflective of the plight of Palestinians in their homeland—struggling to resist settler colonial occupation and still celebrate the joy of family, friends, and their ability to survive. An essential read for educators and students trying to understand the Palestinian fight to hold onto home."

—**Samia Shoman, Northern California high school social studies teacher and district leader for ethnic studies implementation**

"Beginning with a calamity—the collapse of a Palestinian school in Silwan, *Determined to Stay* unearths the struggle to defend the humanity of Palestinian youth and educators, a story that has all too often been buried in the subterrain of American education. By making connections between the experiences of Palestinian youth and African American youth, this book is a critical resource for explaining the Palestinian struggle to young people in the US."

—**Jesse Hagopian, ethnic studies educator, editor of *Teaching for Black Lives***

"In an accessible and engrossing narrative, *Determined to Stay* offers students—and the rest of us—a rare opportunity to hear Palestinian youth and their families talk about their lives. Most exciting are the many connections drawn between how young people experience colonial conquest in the United States and in Palestine, and the focus on resistance. This wonderful book is the perfect introduction to Palestine and why it matters. It's also a deep and thoughtful exploration of one village—Silwan—for those already knowledgeable about Palestine."

—Roxanne Dunbar-Ortiz, author of *Not "a Nation of Immigrants":*
Settler Colonialism, White Supremacy, and a History of Erasure and Exclusion
and *An Indigenous Peoples' History of the United States*

"'What is life like for you?' Jody Sokolower asks the children and young people of the Palestinian village of Silwan. Her extraordinary book tells their stories—children living under occupation being arrested and harassed by Israeli soldiers, young Palestinian-Americans resisting the erasure of their people in US schools, the Madaa youth center where music from traditional debka to hip-hop provides the soundtrack for Palestinian kids' lives. And she brings the stories home, documenting the parallel histories in which Israeli efforts to destroy Palestinian lives and seize their land are met with the same generations of resistance as US efforts to eliminate the Indigenous people of this land."

—Phyllis Bennis, author of *Understanding the Palestinian-Israeli Conflict*

"*Determined to Stay* is a critically important counter-story to the current curriculum being taught in K-12 schools. Linking the histories of settler-colonialism in Palestine and the US, Sokolower uses *testimonios* to humanize the complex and interconnected stories of resistance, building a platform for solidarity across continents that have endured the similar violent tactics resulting in intergenerational trauma, land loss and cultural erasure. Through the voices of the youth and adults of Silwan and Indigenous activists in California, this book offers us an opportunity to make connections and reimagine a future that includes the return of land back to its original people. A must-read for students, teachers and teacher educators!"

—Anita Fernández, Co-Founder and Director of the Xicanx Institute for
Teaching and Organizing

DETERMINED TO STAY
PALESTINIAN YOUTH FIGHT
FOR THEIR VILLAGE

JODY SOKOLOWER
INTRODUCTION BY NICK ESTES

OLIVE
BRANCH
PRESS

An imprint of Interlink Publishing Group, Inc.
www.interlinkbooks.com

First published in 2021 by

Olive Branch Press
An imprint of Interlink Publishing Group, Inc.
46 Crosby Street, Northampton, MA 01060
www.interlinkbooks.com

Published in association with Middle East Children's Alliance, Berkeley, California

Library of Congress Cataloging-in-Publication data available
ISBN-13: 978-1-62371-888-6

Printed and bound in the United States of America

To the children and youth of Silwan

CONTENTS

Nick Estes is a citizen of the Lower Brule Sioux Tribe and cofounder of Red Nation, an Indigenous resistance organization. An assistant professor in the American Studies Department at the University of New Mexico, Estes is the author of Our History Is the Future: Standing Rock Versus the Dakota Access Pipeline and the Long Tradition of Indigenous Resistance and co-editor of Standing with Standing Rock: Voices from the #NoDAPL Movement.

INTRODUCTION
"WE HAVE TO TALK ABOUT PALESTINE AND TURTLE ISLAND IN THE SAME BREATH"

by Nick Estes

When I was a young child, four or five years old, my father took me to the shoreline of the Missouri River, Mni Sose, and pointed out into the water where our home was before my grandfather and grandmother's lands were drowned by the US Army Corps of Engineers. They flooded our land to build the Big Bend Dam, which brought a reservoir and hydroelectricity to the surrounding white communities. My people, the Lower Brule Sioux, were forced from our homes in the bottom lands of the Missouri River Valley.

In that moment, even though I was only a child, I realized that settler colonialism isn't only about taking land. It is also about destroying our land and our connection to it. They could have built that dam anywhere on the Missouri River, but they chose the location of our reservation because they saw our land as disposable, just like they saw our people.

As I grew up, my father, my grandfather, and other relatives told me what the land was like before it was flooded. People could go to the river to drink the water and pick berries. Entire families subsisted on the free goods of nature: wild fruits and herbs, hunting, and fishing. Families would harvest what they called mouse beans and plants that we used for medicine. Some folks had herds of cattle to feed our community and make some money.

When the US invaded Iraq and called it "Indian Country," I realized that something happening on the other side of the world was connected to our Lakota history.

When the dam was built, all that disappeared. About a third of our people had to move. They were pushed off the reservation and forced to "integrate" into the surrounding white communities, where the white people acted as though they wanted our land but they didn't want us as people.

So I grew up in Chamberlain, South Dakota, thirty miles downriver. It's what we call a border town. Border towns are white-dominated settlements that ring Indian reservations, where persistent patterns of racism and discrimination against Indigenous people define everyday life. At school, most of the history I learned was the mainstream kind of flag-waving patriotism, and that was hard for me as a Native youth. It would have helped me so much to learn about Palestine, to be able to see the connections between what has happened to my people and what is happening to the people of Palestine. It would have helped me understand our history and helped me feel stronger in the fight to reclaim it and the land that has been taken from us.

When the US invaded Iraq in 2003, I began to understand that the invasion was a continuation of the Indian wars. I remember watching television and hearing the reporter talk about missiles being launched into "Indian country"—that's what they called Iraq. I thought, "Wow, they haven't even changed the language." That was when I realized that something happening on the other side of the world was connected to our Lakota history.

Once I got to the University of South Dakota, I went to hear a guest speaker, American Indian Movement (AIM) leader Madonna Thunder Hawk. She talked about AIM's relationship to struggles in Northern Ireland, apartheid South Africa, and Palestine. She told us that the Palestine Liberation Organization's fight for the United Nations to recognize Palestinians as a colonized people created a pathway for us to gain the same recognition. That's when I began to see the parallels between Israel and the United States.

I finally got to visit Palestine in 2019. One thing that shocked me was the intensity, speed, and aggression of how Israeli settlers are taking over Palestinian land. And how, similar to US history, so much of that theft is "legal"—mandated by Israeli laws and approved by Israeli courts. For example, Indians weren't US citizens until 1924. We couldn't own property. We needed a pass to leave the reservation. We needed a permit to improve our land or to run cattle. In *Determined to Stay*, you'll see a parallel story unfolding in Silwan, as the Israelis use racist laws to push more and more Palestinians out of the village. And you'll read the best part of the story: Silwani kids and their families talking about how they are fighting to stay.

Israeli and US land policies are based on similar myths. There is an Israeli slogan that was used to raise money in the United States: "Israel is making the desert bloom." But Palestinians have been growing sustainable crops for thousands of years; it is Israeli land policies that are destroying the aquifers, uprooting 1,000-year-old olive trees, and wrecking the fragile ecosystems of the area. That happened here in the United States, too. Given what most of us learn in school, when you think of Native people, you probably think of buffalo hunters and nomadic people. You don't think of agriculture, but 80 percent of Indigenous cultures in the Western Hemisphere were farmers and agriculturalists, growing corn (we invented corn!), squash, beans, and potatoes.

I wasn't able to go to Silwan, but I did go to the Old City in Jerusalem. My mom has passed away, but as a Christian she always wanted to visit the Holy City. So it was important to me to visit it in her memory. At many of the archeological sites in the Old City and throughout Palestine, there were Israeli experts giving completely different versions of the history than what the Palestinian experts were explaining to us. That is why I find the story of King David National Park, one of the central themes of *Determined to Stay*, so fascinating. It reminds me of tourists coming to our sacred sites.

For example, recently I took a group of people to Wind Cave—our place of origin in the Black Hills, which we call *He Sapa*. But I cannot go to our site of creation, which is a holy and spiritual place to us, without the presence of a US park ranger. And, by law, the park ranger has to tell the official park version of the history, even in front of Indigenous people. They tell a sanitized, make-believe history of the park and of the land itself. So I had to stand there and listen to the ranger before I could teach my group about our true history. We can't even go to pray there without permission. We have to get passes, and sometimes you have to register a year in advance.

One of the places we visited in Palestine was al-Lydd, which reminded me of the border towns near my reservation. It is considered part of Israel, but has a large Palestinian population—a very poor Palestinian population. When we arrived, our bus pulled into a parking lot. Our host looked troubled as he came up to the bus and the bus driver opened the door. Stepping in, he introduced himself. We followed him out of the bus and began to form a circle.

Suddenly, he started to cry. "I apologize for crying," he said, "but where you parked the bus is the site of a mass grave." During the *Nakba*,[1] he told us, the Israeli army came to this town. Some people fled, but many stayed and took refuge in one of the mosques. About 250 people, mostly old men, women, and children, stayed in this mosque for two weeks. At the end of two weeks, the Israeli soldiers didn't want to guard the mosque any longer, so they lobbed grenades into it and killed everyone inside. Then they paid villagers who had escaped to clear out the bodies and bury them in a ditch. They paved over the ditch and turned it into a parking lot. Our host showed us diaries and testimony

....

1   Nakba means "catastrophe" in Arabic. It refers to the 1947-48 violent expulsion of 750,000 Palestinians from their homes and land as part of the formation of the state of Israel.

from Israeli soldiers documenting what had happened.

Much of our Native history, too, has been paved over. In *Determined to Stay*, you'll read about the West Berkeley Shellmound in California, an Ohlone burial ground that was paved over to become a parking lot, and the fight to turn it back into sacred space. You'll also read an eerily similar story about an African burial ground in New York City.

What I experienced in Palestine was a deeper sense of what resistance feels like.

Being in Palestine changed my life. I wasn't in doubt about the facts of Palestinian history when I went. What I experienced was a deeper sense of what resistance feels like. I've done land defense work at Standing Rock and in the Navajo Nation. Wherever there is occupation, there is resistance. There is always something beautiful about the sense of freedom in a shared struggle. But I was amazed at the level of resistance among everyday Palestinians, from young children to elders. There's a far greater consciousness around the illegality and the immorality of the occupation than here in the United States. We can all learn so much from their experiences and their determination.

Israel is smaller than the state of New Jersey and it has only existed as a country for a little more than 70 years. What we call Manifest Destiny here in the United States is still happening at breakneck speed in Israel, but there they call it the Promised Land. As Indigenous people in the United States, we have become foreigners on our own land; Israeli textbooks actually call Palestinians "travelers" instead of calling them Palestinians! Each situation helps explain the other. We have to talk about Palestine and Turtle Island[2] in the same breath.

To understand the United States you have to see it not just from the story it tells about itself, but from the perspectives of

....
2   Turtle Island is an Indigenous and First Nations' name for what the US calls North America.

the people it has tried to eliminate, assimilate, and enslave. The same is true for Israel. We have to learn about it, not only from the story it tells about itself, but from the stories the Palestinians tell. Focusing on just one village, Silwan, is a way to hear those Palestinian voices.

PART I:
WELCOME TO SILWAN

Palestine (Israel) is on the eastern shore of the Mediterranean Sea, at the crossroads of Eurasia, North Africa, and the Arabian Peninsula. (Credit: iStock/Henry Bortman)

Palestine and neighboring countries. (Credit: iStock/Henry Bortman)

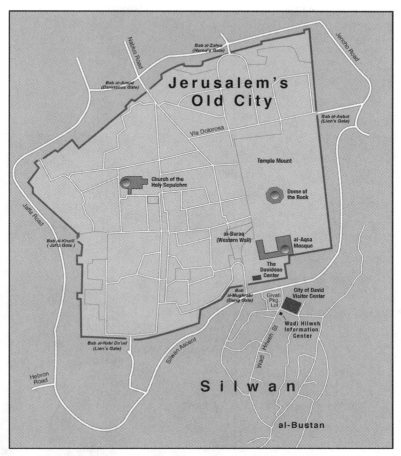

The Old City and Silwan in eastern Jerusalem. (Credit: Jan de Jong/Passia/Henry Bortman)

A mural in Silwan depicts the destruction caused by excavations under Wadi Hilweh neighborhood and the Old City. (Credit: Alternative Information Center)

I
A CLASSROOM FALLS INTO A TUNNEL

February 1, 2009, was a cloudy day in Silwan, a Palestinian village just south of the Old City in Jerusalem. Students at the United Nations school for girls were sitting in their fifth-period classes. Some were listening to their teacher, some were teasing their friends or daydreaming as they looked out the window.

Suddenly, there was a horrible cracking noise. An entire classroom—students, teacher, desks, books, backpacks—fell into the cellar. The air was filled with the screams of the frightened and injured girls. People from the neighborhood came running to see what had happened and to help. Seventeen girls went to the hospital, several of them seriously injured.

"I have been a teacher here at the school for twenty-five years," a woman told the TV cameras when they arrived at the school. She was wearing a white hijab[3] and a heavy blue coat against the winter chill. "The weakness in the school, the reason it collapsed, is because of the excavations [the Israelis] are making under our neighborhood."

"No, that isn't true," interrupted Nir Barkat, the Israeli mayor of Jerusalem. In a stylish suit and expensive haircut, he cut off the teacher and tried to pull the TV cameras back to him.

"Homes in Silwan are collapsing," yelled the teacher. "Wadi Hilweh Street has fallen in twice, the mosque has flooded, there

....
3   Hijab is a head covering worn in public by many Muslim women.

Silwan is at the center of the conflict over whether Jerusalem is an Israeli city or a Palestinian city.

are landslides. This is because they are digging tunnels right under our houses and schools—they don't even tell us it is happening. Someone could be killed."

"That is not the problem," Barkat replied dismissively. "It's just the rains."

More than a decade later, the school is still too dangerous to use, and those tunnels aren't a secret. In fact, they are advertised all over the world as an Israeli theme park—The City of David—and filled with a half million visitors every year. The collapse of the UN school was an early warning sign that Israel had big plans for Silwan—plans that threaten the existence of the Palestinian community.

Silwan is at the center of the conflict over whether Jerusalem is an Israeli city or a Palestinian city. When then-President Trump announced in January 2018 that he was moving the US embassy from Tel Aviv to Jerusalem, he threw US support behind Israel's claims to the city, despite international law that forbids Israeli occupation of Jerusalem.

Areen, a sixteen-year-old Silwani teenager, explained the impact on Palestinian residents:

"Both my mother's family and my father's family have been here for hundreds of years, but now our lives are unbearable. There is always Israel and what they do to us, what they do to our neighbors. We are always afraid of what will happen. The police stop us all the time: going to school, coming from the mosque, whenever we are on the street. Every time I think, 'Maybe I will die today. Or maybe I will continue my life.'

"Life in Jerusalem is especially unbearable for girls like me, who wear full hijab. The Israelis have an idea that we are all terrorists. A friend of mine, she didn't do anything, she was just walking home from school. The Israeli police stopped her and started swearing at her. They searched her.

"She told them, 'I have to go home. It's late. My parents won't know where I am.' But they took her to Room #4 at the Russian Compound—that's an Israeli central police station where they interrogate people—and they didn't release her until the next day. Can you imagine the stress, the feelings her parents had when they didn't know where she had gone or what had happened?

"The peaceful life that our great-grandparents lived in Palestine doesn't exist now. And peace is something every person needs to live their life in a good way."

I met Areen on a recent trip to Silwan. I first visited the village in 2012 and have been back several times since. I'm a teacher, so my students are always on my mind when I'm in Palestine. There are many differences between Palestine and the United States, but what strikes me most are the similarities. Areen's comments reminded me of one of my students, Michael. Michael is African American and grew up in Berkeley, California. One day in class we were discussing the impact of the prison system on Black communities in the United States. Michael said: "I feel like I have a bullseye on my back. Every man in my family has spent time in prison. Some days I think no matter how hard I work in school, how careful I am in the street, I'm going to end up there, too."

That's how children in Silwan feel, too. In all my conversations with youth there, I never met a boy older than eight who hadn't been arrested at least once.

2
MY PATH TO SILWAN

As a white, Jewish, high school social studies teacher, I was critical of how Israel treated Palestinians, but for a long time, I didn't teach about Palestine. It wasn't in the curriculum, and there were too many other important things to cover. The administration already thought I was a troublemaker, and I worried I would get fired. And besides, would my students think Palestine mattered?

Then a young colleague of mine told me that an Israeli and a Palestinian teenager were coming to talk to his classes. Would my World History classes like to join them? My students were interested, so I said yes. We watched the movie *Promises* (which follows the lives of several Palestinian and Israeli teenagers) and did some background reading. My students had read Elie Wiesel's *Night* in their English classes, so they knew about the Holocaust from his first-person account. Most knew about the founding of the State of Israel in 1948, a few years after the end of World War II. But many of them didn't realize that Palestinians were already living on that land. They didn't know that 750,000 Palestinians were forced to leave their homes in 1948, or that Palestinians are still living under an illegal occupation.

The day of the event, we crowded into my colleague's classroom. The visitors introduced themselves. They had both participated in a summer camp in Maine, where the goal was for Palestinian and Israeli youth to see each other as individuals. They were proud that they could calmly discuss their different perspectives. First the

Israeli youth described her family and school, and then she told us about a bus that exploded in Jerusalem—a Palestinian police officer had detonated a bomb on the bus, killing himself and ten Israeli passengers. "We were terrified," she said. "I ride that bus all the time. That's why Israel needs a wall—to protect us from the Palestinians. Everything Israel does is so we can be safe."

Then the Palestinian youth told us about his life in a village near Bethlehem. His neighborhood was surrounded by checkpoints; the Israelis were building a wall that cut his family off from their olive trees and vegetable garden. His father had spent many years in an Israeli prison. "The Israelis say that we are terrorists," he told us. "But we only want to live in peace. They have taken our land, and now we live like prisoners even when we have done nothing wrong."

Afterwards, my students had lots of questions:

"How did things get to be so bad between the Israelis and the Palestinians?"

"When I listened to the Israeli girl, I thought she was right. But then, when I heard the Palestinian guy, I thought he was right. How do I figure this out?"

"How will this end?"

"What can we do to help?"

I tried to answer their questions, but I realized how little I knew about Palestine. So I reached out for help. I contacted Zeiad Abbas Shamrouch, a Palestinian educator who grew up in a refugee camp near Bethlehem and is now executive director of the Middle East Children's Alliance (MECA). MECA is based in Berkeley, California, where I live. I asked him to come talk to my students.

Soon Zeiad and I were working together, leading workshops for teachers on Palestine. Zeiad uses his own family's history to explain what's happening in Palestine today, and I talk about how to turn that into lessons and units. But I still had lots of questions. Zeiad told me, "You need to go see for yourself."

So I did. My partner, Karen, and our daughter Ericka, who was in college then, came with me on that first trip. Colleagues from MECA put us in touch with friends and family to guide our journey. We visited Dheisheh, the refugee camp near Bethlehem where Zeiad grew up; we went to Jerusalem and Hebron and Ramallah. The trip had a profound effect on all of us.

I got back to school, Ericka wrote in her journal, and it was just classes, homework, and parties as usual. At school, who's right—the Palestinians or the Israelis—was a debate. But in Palestine, it was so clear that Palestinians are living under the worst kind of oppression. I saw apartheid[4] first-hand, a different aspect in every city we visited: In Bethlehem, Israel's apartheid wall makes a big loop right through the center of the city, cutting Palestinians off from their families, schools, hospitals, and

....
4   Apartheid was a system of institutionalized segregation based on race in South Africa. The term is often used to describe Israel's similar system of racialized discrimination and separation.

Children in East Jerusalem look over the apartheid wall at an Israeli settlement.

"Palestinians don't have the same legal rights as Israelis; everything is segregated. It reminds me of what I learned about Jim Crow in the South."

their olive groves. In Hebron, Israeli settlers have built houses right on top of the only Palestinian market street in Hebron's Old City that hasn't been closed down, and they throw garbage down on the shoppers and the market stalls. We saw the home of one Palestinian family that has to climb in and out of their back window because they aren't allowed to go out their front door—that street is for Israelis only.

Everywhere in the West Bank, there are separate roads for Israelis and tourists that Palestinians can't use; they even have different license plates. For Palestinians, water is rationed and very expensive. You can always spot a Palestinian house by the water storage tank on the roof. Israelis, even those living right next door to Palestinians, have unlimited water. They have swimming pools and gardens and wash their cars. Some of them shoot holes in the Palestinians' water tanks for target practice. The schools are separate; Palestinians don't have the same legal rights as Israelis; everything is segregated. It reminds me of what I learned about Jim Crow in the South.

Like Ericka, I was shocked at how the Israeli occupation affects every part of Palestinian life. And I struggled with intense feelings throughout our trip. The Palestinians we met—tour guides, cab drivers, community organizers, shop owners—were generous and kind. They told us over and over that the fault lay with the US government, not with the people of the United States; that the problem was Israel, not Judaism. But it was hard not to feel a toxic stew of anger and guilt after meeting Zeiad's niece, who gave me a beaded necklace she made while in an Israeli prison, or facing the apartheid wall that snakes through Bethlehem, splitting the city into shattered pieces.

Our visit to Hebron was the hardest for me. Our guide took us to visit a family of farmers whose land was completely surrounded by Israeli fences and guard towers. The Israeli settlers barged onto their land to erect tents and hold Jewish services; sharpshooters in the guard towers shot at them when they tried to take care of their animals or harvest their olives. Then we went to visit a family in the city center whose house had been attacked by the settlers; one of their children was killed. They showed us the bullet holes in the bedroom wall, and the bullet holes through the water tanks on their roof. There were Israeli soldiers with Uzi machine guns in their hands everywhere. By the time we left Hebron, I was shaking.

The next day, we went to Silwan.

Silwan (in the foreground) and the walled Old City. The large dome is the golden Dome of the Rock, a UNESCO World Heritage Site and the most recognizable landmark in Jerusalem. (Credit: UPI/Alamy)

3
"AHLAN!" WELCOME TO SILWAN

People have been living in Silwan since 5,000 BCE (7,000 years ago). For many of those years, it was a resting place for travelers just before they got to the gated Old City of Jerusalem. Because of the Silwan Spring (Ein Silwan in Arabic), it was a lush picnic spot for people in the area, with cool running water and shady caves to explore in the hot summers. The spring also meant there was water for irrigation, so Silwan was called the "breadbasket of Jerusalem." Food grown in the village supplied the fruit and vegetable sellers in the markets of the Old City.

The Old City is the heart of Jerusalem. It's a walled city within the city that dates back to Biblical times. There are stone-paved streets, ancient towers and covered, winding passageways. It's the home of important religious sites: the Temple Mount and Western Wall for Jews, the Church of the Holy Sepulchre and the Via Dolorosa for Christians, the Dome of the Rock and al-Aqsa Mosque for Muslims. But it's also home to thousands of Palestinians, and more and more Jewish settlers[5]. The narrow walkways are lined with shops and restaurants. People buying spices or cell phones bump up against tourists looking for the

....

5   A major aspect of Israel's strategy for claiming all of Jerusalem is offering incentives to Jews to move into Palestinian neighborhoods, including those in Silwan and in the Old City. Palestinians see these people as illegal settlers, just as Native Americans saw the Europeans who forced them off their lands and then built settlements to claim the space.

Silwan is a village with two realities.

best falafel, Christian pilgrims singing as they walk from one Station of the Cross to the next, and Muslims hurrying to prayers.

There are six gates into the Old City. The one at the south end of the city is called the *Mughrabi* (Moroccan) Gate. It's also called the Dung Gate because the garbage dump for the city used to be nearby.

Silwan starts just beyond the Mughrabi Gate. The Israelis see control of the Old City and the area around it as central to their plans to make Jerusalem the capital of Israel. Because Silwan is so close to the Old City, the Israelis are trying to force Palestinians to leave the village. But the Silwanis are determined to stay.

So Silwan is a village with two realities. Karen, Ericka, and I could see those two realities within minutes of our first visit there. We took a taxi from our hotel near the Damascus Gate. We drove around the perimeter of the Old City walls and got dropped off in front of the Mughrabi Gate. We crossed the street, crowded with Israeli tour buses and taxis, and entered the village of Silwan.

City of David National Park entrance.
(Credit: ©Alefbet26 Dreamstime.com)

On the right side of the street was a large excavation site: a big hole in the ground honeycombed with scaffolding, wooden stairways, and plank bridges. The site was surrounded by a wire fence hung with murals showing happy children learning about archeology. Peering through the fence, we could see college-aged youth in small groups, working on the site. We wondered what they were digging up. Beyond the excavation, small houses lined the sides of Wadi Hilweh Street as it sloped sharply downhill.

A few steps down the left side of the street, we saw the entrance to Israel's City of David National Park. Brand new stone walls that mimic Old City architecture towered over the front gate, which was adorned with a gilded golden harp—the symbol of King David—and gold lettering in Hebrew and English. Flowering plants covered the walls.

"The City of David is an archeological Disneyland."

According to the Bible, David was a musician, military leader, and poet about 3,000 years ago. He killed the giant Goliath with a slingshot and was recognized as a great fighter. After he was appointed king of the Jewish people, he conquered the city of Jerusalem and made it the center of his realm. Many Israelis use the Biblical story of David as the basis for saying that Jerusalem should be the capital of present-day Israel.

We walked past the heavily armed guards and into the open-air plaza. It was bustling: there were Israeli teenage soldiers with rifles slung over their shoulders; grade-school classes; and tour groups from all over the world, chatting excitedly in half a dozen languages. We could have bought tickets for a rainbow assortment of tours exploring the tunnels underneath Silwan, watched a 3D movie about King David's kingdom, or signed up for a City of David paint-ball party.

"We're in an archeological Disneyland," Ericka said.

We didn't buy any tickets. Instead, we left the City of David and walked a few doors down the street to a small building with a battered red metal door propped open with a rock. The sign above the door said "Wadi Hilweh Information Center." There was a hand-lettered poster on the wall that read: "I Love You Silwan!" We had come to visit the center of a very different perspective on the neighborhood: that of Palestinians living in a village under siege.

Three little girls, four or five years old, came running out to welcome us.

Entrance to the Wadi Hilweh Information Center, also home of the Madaa Creative Center. (Credit: Nihad Siyam)

"*Marhaba*," we said carefully. "Hello" in Arabic, marhaba was one of the few things we could say in Palestine's home language.

"*Ahlan*," the girls responded. "Welcome." They led us into the center, where Jawad Siyam, the founding director of the center, thanked the girls and invited us into his office. Tall and thin, Jawad looked exhausted, but he greeted us warmly and went to make coffee for us. Coffee in Palestine is thick, dark, and served in tiny cups.

"The City of David looks so out of place on Wadi Hilweh Street," we said to Jawad. "What is it doing here?"

"The City of David Park was created by a development company called Elad," he explained. "Really, Elad is the reason we have the Wadi Hilweh Information Center.

"Palestine has been under Israeli occupation since before I was born, but when I was a child, Silwan was a Palestinian village. I had to leave the country to go to university in the 1990s; when I returned, Silwan was filled with Israeli settlers. They were buying houses, stealing houses, building on Palestinian land. Elad was behind all of it. They were tunneling under the neighborhood, recruiting settlers and building settlements[6]. They built the City of David as a tourist attraction that promotes the view that all of Jerusalem, including Silwan, is and was always a Jewish city.

"I was shocked. By 2003, I saw that they did not want any kind of Palestinian life here in Silwan. They were trying to make all of us leave the village. So I started to think about how to make the Palestinian community stronger, to bring us together. We started creating activities, especially with the kids. We had summer games, we cleaned the streets, did volunteer work. Finally, we started the Wadi Hilweh Information Center and the Madaa Creative Center. The Madaa Creative Center is for the children. Come, let me show you around."

"Here, in this building, along with the information center, we have the Madaa library, art and music classes, and the computer lab." The computer lab was a small room ringed with computers on low tables. All the computers had children playing on them; a few others waited their turns. Jawad translated a sign in Arabic that told the children they could use the computer for thirty minutes before giving another child a turn. In the library, a young woman was drawing pictures with a group of preschool children. Jawad's office was the headquarters of the information center, which reports on Israeli attacks on the community and community resistance.

Jawad took us to another building behind the center. It was the home of Madaa's women's classes. When we walked in, the teacher, a middle-aged woman wearing a thawb[7] and hijab, explained that the women were learning to make mosaic table tops.

....

6   Israeli settlements are communities of Israeli citizens, almost exclusively of Jewish ethnicity, built on lands designated as Palestinian in the Oslo Accords, which Israel signed in 1993. In 2004, the International Court of Justice declared these settlements illegal under international law.

7   Thawb is a floor-length traditional Palestinian women's dress. It is black and long-sleeved. Often the front panel and sleeves are hand-embroidered.

They hoped that this skill would be a way to earn money, which is very difficult in Silwan, especially for women. The teacher showed us what they were doing: They created a geometric design, then traced it on a square piece of wood. Small pieces of colored pottery were arranged, upside down, to fill in the design. When the design was complete, caulk was applied to hold it together, then a wood backing. Finally, the completed mosaic was flipped over so the design was right-side up. The table tops were beautiful.

None of the women spoke English, so we were dependent on Jawad to translate. But the women's pride in their work didn't need translation. They all hugged us as we got ready to go.

"Now," said Jawad, "let me show you our newest success. We have just been able to open a cultural café."

He led us across the street. The front yard of the café was a playground. Far to one side there was a small stable with two horses and a goat. Inside, the café was a big, light-filled room with a kitchen at one end and tables, chairs, and padded benches at the other. The tables had mosaic tops made by the women's group at the center. The murals on the walls had been painted by artists from around the world who came to visit Silwan. One of them echoed the sign we had seen outside the information center: "I Love You Silwan!"

Jawad told us that the staff, who brought us coffee and pastries, had all been in Israeli prisons. "Once you've been arrested or spent time in prison, it's almost impossible to find a job here," he said.

"That's true in the United States, too," Karen said. "Once you've been incarcerated, the punishment goes on and on."

"The cultural café is a place where people from the village can come and relax," Jawad continued. "We show movies, host community events. We have soccer and volleyball teams practicing on the playground. We'll use this for our summer camp. There are so few places in Silwan to have fun; families come here to enjoy themselves."

"Can you tell us about the 'I love you Silwan' mural? I saw the poster by the entrance to Madaa," Ericka said.

"You'll see that on walls all over Silwan," Jawad said. "The Israelis won't allow us to fly the Palestinian flag, even though you see Israeli flags everywhere. So we write 'I love you Silwan' instead."

"The Israelis won't allow us to fly the Palestinian flag. So we write 'I love you Silwan' instead."

We thanked Jawad, hugged him goodbye, and headed back up the hill to the bus and our hotel. It was almost time for us to head back to the United States, and we were glad that our day in Silwan was near the end of our trip. Silwan was special: It felt full of hope in a situation that often seemed filled with losses and pain. When we returned to the United States, we told all our friends about Silwan.

Only two weeks after we got back, one of those friends sent me a link. "Isn't this the village you told me about?" she asked. I opened the link to a news article from the Israeli newspaper *Haaretz*: On February 13, 2012, the Israeli Nature and Parks Authority bulldozed the cultural café, destroying it completely. There was no sign of the horses or the goat.

Israeli backhoe destroying the cultural café. (Credit: Wadi Hilweh Information Center)

I was horrified. How could the Israelis destroy a community center just like that? And why did so few people in the United States know what was happening? I couldn't pretend this had nothing to do with me. The United States gives $3.8 billion a year to Israel. When we were walking around Silwan, I noticed that many of the Israeli settlers were speaking English with New York accents like mine.

After talking with Zeiad, I decided to return to Silwan, interview teenagers and other members of the community, and write about the village. Palestine can seem so far away and US media makes it seem like the issues are too complicated to understand. Maybe, I thought, I can use the story of this one village to help make clear what's really going on. I wanted to write about Silwan as a way to help youth in the United States understand what is happening in Palestine, and to demonstrate the connections it has to US history and to what's happening in the United States today.

Silwani children playing soccer in front of the demolished cultural café. (Credit: Madaa Creative Center)

Those connections are clear to many Palestinian youth. When demonstrations broke out in Ferguson, Missouri, over the 2014 killing of unarmed Michael Brown, the police responded with tear gas, night sticks, and rubber bullets. Activists in Palestine were among the first to offer solidarity and suggestions, especially when they realized that the same tear gas canisters—made in the United States—were being used in both places: "Solidarity with #Ferguson," tweeted Mariam Barghouti from the West Bank. "Always make sure to run against the wind and to keep calm when you're teargassed, the pain will pass, don't rub your eyes!" Rana Nazzal tweeted, "#Palestine knows what it means to be shot for your ethnicity."

The Damascus Gate to the Old City in Jerusalem. (Credit: Madaa Youth Photography Program)

4
ERICKA AND I HEAD BACK TO SILWAN

By the time I was able to return to Silwan, Ericka had graduated from college and was between jobs, so she agreed to come and take photographs.

We talked with colleagues at MECA about how to approach our project, and Zeiad and I talked on the phone with Jawad. Jawad was excited that we wanted to focus on youth. "We will help you all we can," he said.

Ericka and I agreed that our interviews and research would be based in Palestinian reality. We weren't going to pretend to be "even-handed" about what was happening in Silwan—we both felt strongly that the Palestinians were fighting against a clear injustice. As US historian Howard Zinn said, "You can't be neutral on a moving train."

We also wanted to support the international campaign to boycott Israeli goods, as a way to show solidarity with Palestine.[8] As much as possible, we would stick to Palestinian hotels, Palestinian restaurants, and Palestinian products.

The only Palestinian airport was destroyed by Israeli bombs many years ago, so visitors have to come in through the Israeli airport at Tel Aviv, or fly to Jordan and cross the Allenby Bridge over the Jordan River. Folks at MECA thought that, as a Jewish family, our chances of getting into Palestine were best going through Tel

8   For more information about the International Campaign to Boycott, Divest from and Sanction Israel (BDS), see chapters 19 and 32.

"If I grew up in Israel, told from elementary school that I needed to defend my country from Palestinian 'terrorists,' would that be me with an Uzi on my shoulder?"

Aviv, so that's what we did. Just a few months earlier, a friend of mine who wanted to do a public health project in Bethlehem had been turned away at the airport; Israeli customs agents found information about her on the internet that revealed that she was critical of Israel. If Israel thinks you support Palestinian rights, they often won't let you enter. So we spent a lot of time cleaning anything about Palestine off our phones and my computer. And, despite our commitment not to spend money in Israel, we decided to stay one night in a Tel Aviv hotel so we could tell the customs agents we were visiting Israel, not Palestine.

We had to take three planes to get to the Tel Aviv airport: from San Francisco to Los Angeles, from Los Angeles to Istanbul, and from Istanbul to Tel Aviv. It took twenty hours. We arrived in Tel Aviv at 2 AM. We didn't have problems with customs but, after a long delay, we learned that our luggage was lost. Dejected and exhausted, we took a cab to our hotel. The next morning the hotel receptionist told us how to get the train to Jerusalem.

Ericka wrote: *It was the first day of Passover vacation, and the railway station was filled with Israeli teenagers, in a rainbow of different military uniforms, carrying automatic rifles. Some of them were high school students in the Israeli version of ROTC[9], but most were 18- and 19-year-olds doing their required two years of military service. None of the other travelers seemed worried that they were surrounded by armed troops. To me, police and soldiers are a dangerous authority. But to the Israelis around me, the soldiers represented safety and security. And they were younger than me. If I grew up in Israel, told from elementary school that I needed to defend my country from Palestinian "terrorists," would that be me with an Uzi on my shoulder?*

....

9   The US Reserve Officer Training Corps (ROTC) is a high school and college program that funnels students into the US military.

Ericka caught up on sleep while the train rumbled by one Israeli settlement after another. We took a bus from the train and the bus driver, the first Palestinian we had met so far, enlisted a friend to show us how to get from the bus stop to the Damascus Gate of the Old City. He took us through back alleys, where we could see young Israeli children playing behind high security fences. Finally, climbing over rocks and concrete in a deserted lot, we could see the walls of the Old City.

Ericka wrote: *Walking into the Old City was the first time I truly felt like we had left the West. Barely any sunlight makes its way into the narrow streets and the ancient paving stones are treacherously smooth. It is loud inside, echoing voices selling everything from baby clothes and chess sets to spices sculpted into huge gold-and-russet pyramids, and more religious iconography than I had ever seen. We wove our way past groups of Christian tourists, recognizable by their bright, matching t-shirts and enthusiastic tour guides. Young Jewish school children were walking to school, flanked by their private armed guards. Unlike the relaxed air of the teenage soldiers at the railway station, these guards kept their hands on the triggers of their weapons. Their heads swiveled back and forth, constantly scanning the crowd from behind their mirrored sunglasses.*

We were staying at the Lutheran Guesthouse in the middle of the Old City. Following a map we had brought with us, we walked up steep stone stairways and down narrow passages.

I was convinced we were totally lost. "Let's ask someone," I said.

"I know where we are," Ericka responded.

Two minutes later, I said it again. And again. Ericka ignored me, just kept looking at the map, checking the markers written high on the stone walls in Arabic, Hebrew, and English, and plowing on. And sure enough, eventually we were in front of the entrance to our hotel on St. Mark's Street. It had been a long, winding, and confusing walk. How, we wondered, would our suitcases ever find us here?

We settled in as best we could without our clothes and everything else you bring on a trip. Most of the other guests were German, in Jerusalem for Easter.

The next morning, Ericka woke me up early. Her period had started and the tampons she had carefully packed were in our lost luggage. "I'll go find a drugstore," I offered. "Get Advil, too," she called as I closed the door. The receptionist at the front desk of the guesthouse described how to get to a Palestinian pharmacy near the Jaffa Gate, but when I got there it wasn't open yet. I leaned against the shop's metal shutters to wait.

A few minutes later, a man came up to me and asked if I wanted a tour. I couldn't tell from his accented English whether he was Palestinian or Israeli.

"No," I said. "I'm just waiting for the drugstore to open."

Palestinian shoppers inside the Old City. (Credit: Alamy)

"I can show you how to get to a drugstore that's open now," he said. He took me to the Jaffa Gate and pointed to some stairs across the plaza. "Go down those stairs and turn right. You can't miss it."

I followed his directions. When I reached the bottom, suddenly I was in another universe: a fancy underground Israeli mall, a sanitized, upscale version of the Old City, with wide stone sidewalks, carefully pruned trees and flowers in pots, and an international array of stores: Abercrombie & Fitch, Tommy Hilfiger, North Face, Swarovski, and a supermarket-sized drugstore. No Palestinians anywhere. I hurriedly bought tampons and Advil, and made my way back through the Old City to our room. It was astonishing how easy Israel made it to opt for convenience and familiarity. Next time, I told myself, I would wait for the Palestinian pharmacy to open.

A few hours later, after a breakfast of labna[10], hummus, cheese, olives, pita, and hard-boiled eggs at the guesthouse, we made our way through the Old City toward Silwan. We passed through the Armenian and Jewish quarters—crowded with shoppers, delivery carts, and children on their way to school. We went out a small side gate and around the west side of the Old City walls.

The road by the Mughrabi Gate was mobbed with Israeli buses. Guides waved flags and yelled in Hebrew and English while hundreds of Israeli families poured off the buses on their way to the Western Wall and the City of David National Park.

We turned the corner onto Wadi Hilweh Street and walked past the entrance to the City of David to the Wadi Hilweh Information Center. Before we went into the center, we crossed the street to see what had happened to the cultural café.

Instead of the beautiful café there was a vacant lot, filled with rubbish and surrounded by a chain-link fence. There was no sign of the mosaic-topped tables or the soccer field. We stared sadly

....
10   Labna is yogurt that has been thickened by letting it drain through a strainer until the consistency is between cream cheese and Greek yogurt.

"Everything in Silwan now is about Israel's deliberate effort to push us out of East Jerusalem and our determination to stay."

at the ruins. It had been such an inspiring oasis, so filled with hope and the spirit of the community. The photos of the bulldozed café had been upsetting, but I was still unprepared for the shock of seeing nothing but rubble.

At least Madaa and the information center were still there. Jawad came out of his office to welcome us. We took a quick peek at the children in the computer lab before joining him in his office.

Jawad already knew about my writing project, but Ericka and I wanted to make sure that we were clear about the direction of the book. "What are the most important things for youth and their families back in the United States to understand about Silwan? About Palestine in general?" we asked.

"Everything in Silwan now is about Israel's deliberate effort to push us out of East Jerusalem and our determination to stay," Jawad said. "I would focus on three parts of their strategy: The first is attacking our children, making their lives so hard that parents will leave out of desperation. They arrest our kids over and over again. They also make it almost impossible for them to get an education. Imagine the pressure that puts on us as parents.

"The second is forcing us out of our houses and off our land.

"And the third is the City of David, how they are using archeology to destroy Palestinian

Jawad Siyam.
(Credit: Ericka Sokolower-Shain)

Silwan. But we are resilient. Each time, we are resisting, fighting back."

We were eager to get started. So Jawad introduced us to Sahar. He said she was working with the children who had been arrested and their parents. She could explain the situation to us and introduce us to some of the children.

Sahar Abbasi looking out over central Silwan. (Credit: Rochelle Watson for Art Forces)

5
ISRAELIS ARREST CHILDREN TO MAKE THEIR PARENTS MOVE

Sahar Abbasi, who is the deputy director of Madaa, invited us into her crowded office. In a flowered hijab, a blue tunic, and pants, she radiated warmth; we felt immediately like old friends. As we talked, Sahar was frequently interrupted by children and other staff members. Each time, she stopped and focused all her attention on the request or question, often dashing out of the room to deal with the situation. Then she'd come back, sit down, and pick up her story. She told us she had four children and she had always lived in Silwan.

"Jawad told us that one way the Israelis are pressuring Palestinians to leave Silwan is by making life impossible for children and teenagers," I said. "Can you tell us about that?"

"Of course. Part of my job is to interview every Silwani child who is released from detention to see if they need academic, psychological, or legal help."

"How long have you been doing this?" I asked.

"Since 2011. That year, Silwan was the hottest spot in East Jerusalem. Almost 200 children were arrested in the village, and their ages were younger and younger.

"We heard terrible stories about what was happening to children in Room #4 at the Russian Compound, the central Israeli police station in Jerusalem. Room #4 is where the Israelis interrogate and torture people they have arrested. The children were denied food, water, and access to the bathroom. Even young children had their hands and legs zip-tied for hours. They were humiliated and threatened. Think about the impact this had on them and their families.

"Before that, I was coordinating the women's projects at Madaa. But we realized this was an emergency. We started doing home visits to all the children who had been detained. The original idea was advocacy—to see if the children needed legal help or other services. But the families also wanted to share their stories. They wanted to tell us what was happening to them and their children."

"Can you give us an example?" I asked.

"There is a neighborhood in Silwan called Bustan. Bustan means garden in Arabic. Not very long ago the area was all gardens, and every family had a plot to grow vegetables and fruit. Now that area of Silwan is almost like a refugee camp. It's so crowded that all the houses are connected to each other. From one window you climb into the window of another house, from one roof you can jump onto another.

"A few years ago, the Israelis had just built a new settlement in Bustan, and sometimes our children would throw stones to protest. But one morning, when the children were busy at school the Israelis started throwing teargas and sound bombs,[11] and shooting rubber bullets. We don't know what had provoked them (if anything). The army, the police, the special forces, they all work together, so you can't tell who is doing what. Sometimes it's undercover forces, sometimes it's intelligence forces, sometimes it's the settlers' private guards. They all have the authority to do anything.

"They jumped from one roof to another and finally they were on a roof with an open window, so they entered the house—seven

....

11   A sound bomb is a vehicle-mounted sonic blaster that shoots repeated pulses of sound at people, leaving them dizzy and nauseous. At close range, they can make victims lose their hearing. Sound bombs were also directed at people protesting in the United States after George Floyd was murdered.

fully armed soldiers. And the woman in the house was in the bathroom giving a bath to her daughter with special needs. In our culture, a woman wouldn't be around strangers in short sleeves, without a scarf, but this woman was in her house, in her bathroom, giving a bath.

"For trying to help his mother, he was taken and interrogated for almost ten hours, this five-year-old boy."

"The soldiers opened the bathroom door where her daughter was taking a bath and pushed the mother. Of course she started screaming and shouting. So who came to help? Her small boy, five years old, who was playing outside. He came holding a rock. He just wanted to protect his mother.

"Then the neighbors intervened. They came because they didn't want a woman who was alone in her house to be attacked. So there was a struggle between the neighbors and the soldiers. The neighbors thought it had ended, so they left. But it never ends with them.

"The soldiers came back at four or five the next morning, knocking on the door and saying they wanted the child. The family refused to give him up.

"This is a little child," the family said. "We will never allow this." But the Israelis insisted that in the morning the mother and the child should be at the Russian Compound.

"So they went in at ten. The police finished interrogating this little boy at about eight at night. The mother was kept until midnight.

"They were just people in their own home, they did nothing wrong. The little boy didn't throw anything. His mother was alone. She was screaming, 'What are you doing? I'm almost naked!' For trying to help his mother, he was taken and interrogated for almost ten hours, this five-year-old boy. It wasn't easy for him after that.

"At Madaa, we connected him with a psychologist who helped him for two years. And he was involved in our activities. He came to computer class, art class, whenever we had an activity, he came. It took a while for him to recover from that experience."

"That must have been terrifying for him, and for his whole family," I said. "How is he now?"

"Now he's ten years old. He's doing well, but he was just arrested again. This time he was kidnapped from the street while he was playing with his friends and his cousins. They weren't doing anything provocative, they were just playing. Sometimes the Israelis take the children for hours without telling anyone where they are. They know it's illegal to arrest children who are so young, but they want to intimidate them.

"In this case, the family found out immediately from the other children, so they were able to find their son and the police near the car wash, still in Silwan. His mother and father argued with the police, and they managed to get him back before he ended up at the police station. That was lucky, but he suffered more than enough during that hour."

Sahar gave us a copy of a Madaa report, "The Impact of Child Arrest and Detention." In 2012, Madaa interviewed thirty children from Silwan, ranging from seven to seventeen years old, who had been arrested and detained. According to the study, 63 percent of the children were denied food, water, and restrooms; 77 percent were physically abused; and 87 percent were psychologically abused. Eighty-three percent of the children or their parents had to sign papers in Hebrew, a language that they did not understand.[12]

----

12   Hebrew is the official language of Israel; Palestinians' language is Arabic.

6

"MY FRIEND WAS ARRESTED BECAUSE HE HAD A BROKEN RULER": MOUSSA'S STORY

We wanted to talk directly with some of those kids, so Sahar introduced us to Moussa. He was small for his fourteen years; at first he seemed overwhelmed by the office chair he sat in. He answered the first few questions in whispered monosyllables as Sahar translated for him. But Sahar drew him out and soon he was more comfortable. As he talked, his voice grew louder and more confident. He sat up taller in the chair.

"Tell us about your family," Sahar said.

"I'm the youngest in my family," Moussa told us. "I have six older sisters, and one brother. We live in the 'Ein al-Loza neighborhood of Silwan."

"He is the one who everyone is spoiling with love," Sahar told us.

"Wait," I said. "Did he say that or did you say that?"

"I asked him if he's spoiled and he laughed and said, 'Yes, I'm the spoiled one.'"

"Ask him about his school."

"I go to Ahmed Saleh al-Khaldi School," Moussa said. "I like the teachers, they care about us. But our school was a shelter and then they turned it into a school. The walls are filthy and broken. I'm on the soccer team, but we have to play indoors."

"Why?" I asked.

"The playground got filled with sewage so we can't use it. Sometimes, we find the Israeli police blocking the entrance at the

Palestinian child arrested in Jerusalem by an undercover Israeli policeman dressed as a Palestinian. (Credit: Al-Quds News Agency)

school gates. They search our backpacks. Early this school year, my friend had a broken ruler in his bag. They said it was a weapon, so they took him away to court. He was under home arrest for two months and they fined his family."

"For a broken ruler?" I couldn't believe it.

"Yes. And now he's afraid to hold anything that could make him have to go back to jail."

"How did that experience affect your friend?"

"Because he was under house arrest, he couldn't leave the house, even to go to school. When he came back, he had changed. He lost a lot of time at school and the teachers told him that he might not pass this year, so he will be a year behind. Before he was arrested he was very active. He liked to play and go out with us. Now he just finishes school and goes home. He doesn't go out with his friends."

Sahar asked Moussa if there were any other stories he wanted to tell us. "This book is for kids in the United States. What do you want to tell them about your life? Do you want to tell them about when you got arrested?"

"Ok. When I was six or seven, me and my cousins went to buy falafel. It was about seven in the evening. There were police in the road, far away, but they saw us. We were eating, but they thought we were getting ready to throw rocks at them. They went after us, so we ran up the mountainside. They threw a sound bomb at us and grabbed us.

"I was so scared. I didn't know where they took us or what they were going to do to me. They asked why we were throwing stones, and who was with us. We told them we were not throwing stones and that no one was with us. Some of the questions were in Arabic, but some were in Hebrew. I don't know Hebrew. They didn't hit us, but they hit the table very hard, making a loud noise, to scare us. Finally, at one in the morning, my father came and paid a fine and they let us go."

"Does that mean he has a police file?" I asked Sahar.

"I'm not sure," she said.

"What do you do for fun?" I asked Moussa. "What are your dreams for the future?"

"I want to be a professional soccer player. My favorite player is Messi, and my favorite team is Barcelona, but I like the German team, too. It's hard for me to play, though, because of the settlers and the soldiers. My mother is always worried what will happen to me, so if I have soccer practice, I can only go if it's right by our house."

We thanked Moussa and he went back to working on his homework in the computer center. Talking with him reminded me of a book I read recently: All American Boys, by Jason Reynolds and Brendan Kiely. It's about a Black teenager in the United States who is shot by a police officer in a convenience store while he is looking for his cell phone in his backpack. For me, All American Boys was a window opened on a school and community affected by this kind of racism, and the impact it has on how those kids feel, how well they do in school, and how they see their futures. There are many differences between the problems faced by kids in

Palestine and those in the United States, but there are similarities, too.

I told Sahar what I had been thinking. "Trauma connected to police abuse has been a huge problem for kids in Silwan, too," she said. "Almost all of the children who've been arrested suffer from anxiety afterward; they often have nightmares or can't sleep. Almost half have trouble with schoolwork or drop out altogether. Many are so badly hurt they need medical help. Others lose weight, withdraw from their families and friends, or suffer from bedwetting. It's a terrible situation."

That night, Ericka and I didn't talk much as we walked up the hill and through the Old City to the guesthouse. I kept remembering the sadness in Moussa's eyes as he talked about his friend.

7

"THE SETTLERS STOLE MY GRANDMOTHER'S HOUSE": NIHAD'S STORY

The next day, our goal was to understand the second way the Israelis are trying to force Palestinians out of Silwan and other parts of East Jerusalem: by stealing people's houses and land. As we walked down to Madaa, Ericka and I talked about how people are being forced out of their homes in the Bay Area where we live.

One example is the Mission District in San Francisco, where we lived when Ericka was in elementary school. For tech workers making lots of money in the computer industry, the Mission is a hip place to live—filled with high-end restaurants, trendy bars, and designer clothing boutiques. For the Latinx families who immigrated to the neighborhood, escaping violence and poverty in Mexico and Central America, it has turned from a neighborhood of refuge to a terrifying mix of immigration raids, insanely expensive rents, evictions, and police shootings.

The richer, mostly white people moving into the neighborhood see the Latinx neighborhood folks as a threat. They call 911 to report "suspicious persons," and the results can be tragic. This happened to a young man named Alex Nieto. Alex attended Horace Mann Middle School, where I was a student teacher. One day a few years ago, Alex was eating a burrito in the park near his home before going to his job as a security guard. Four cops, responding to a 911 call from a dogwalker who thought Alex looked

The role the police and other armed forces play in pushing folks out of their neighborhoods is a pattern you can see from San Francisco to Chicago to East Jerusalem.

threatening, sped into the park, fired fifty-seven bullets at Alex, and killed him. The cops were never charged.

Of course, there are differences between the Bay Area and Silwan, but the role the police and other armed forces play in pushing folks out of their neighborhoods is a pattern you can see from San Francisco to Chicago to East Jerusalem.

When we got to Madaa, Jawad introduced us to his brother, Nihad. Nihad is a taxi driver, but his taxi was in the repair shop, so he became our translator for the rest of our trip. We asked him how the Israeli settlers have ended up with so many houses in Silwan.

"Let me tell you about my grandmother's house," he responded. He took us outside, just beyond the center's red door, to point out the house next door. "See the electric gate and the Israeli flag flying from the top? That used to be my grandmother's house. In 1988, my grandmother died. We have Muslim rituals when someone dies: We place the body on the table and we wash it. If the person who died is a woman, women come to wash it; men wash the body of men.

"While the women were washing my grandmother's body, a woman came into the house. She was Palestinian, but we knew she was collaborating with the Israeli authorities and the settlers.[13] She came with an ink pad and six sheets of blank stationery, printed at the top with the name and address of an American lawyer.

"This woman came into the room where they were washing my grandmother's body, inked my grandmother's fingers and pushed her fingerprints onto the stationery.

....

13   The Israelis sometimes pressure Palestinians who have been arrested to work with them (often as spies) in order to avoid prison. Almost everyone refuses, even under torture, but occasionally someone agrees. These people are called collaborators.

"The woman who was washing my grandmother said, 'What are you doing?'

"The collaborator said, 'We have to protect her property because her sons are not here,' and rushed out of the house.

"Then the settlers used those papers to say that my grandmother had agreed to sell her land to the settlers. They typed the agreement above her fingerprint. Before, when many people couldn't write, they used a fingerprint instead of a signature.

Nihad Siyam.
(Credit: Ericka Sokolower-Shain)

"We are fighting this in the courts. The problem is that the court always says 'The situation will stay the way it is now until we resolve it.' The settlers stole my grandmother's house. Now they are inside and have built that strong gate."

"That's outrageous!" I said. "What kind of person would desecrate the body of someone's grandmother to steal her house?"

"This is just one example of how they take our houses. For most of the houses and land here in Silwan, we don't have documents of ownership because we have lived in the same houses, on the same land, for hundreds of years. And they know that.

"Every place that is empty, the settlers force their way inside and then you have to prove that it belongs to your family. If you are Palestinian, you have to prove it is yours. The settlers just go inside and take it, but the original owner has to prove it doesn't belong to the settlers.

"Last week, the settlers got control of another house in our neighborhood. It's a property where there are two houses and the land around it. The settlers had already taken the land and one of the houses. The owner of the land, his sister, and her children lived in the other house.

"The settlers broke into that house and told the owner's sister and her children to get out. They threw them into the street. The settlers said the court gave them documents for the house, but it was not true.

"Many people from the neighborhood came to support the family. We all sat in the street and stopped traffic. The police officers told us to leave. But we said, 'The settlers took their house, so where do you want them to go?'

"Then the special forces arrived. They started kicking people, yelling at us to move. They threw tear gas and sound bombs. They seized a thirteen-year-old boy and tied his hands with zip ties. They said he was under arrest for disturbing their ability to do their job. I tried to take the boy away from them, but they attacked me and the boy's uncle, who was also trying to protect the boy. They grabbed me around my neck and pushed so I couldn't breathe.

"I said, 'Take your hands off me, I didn't do anything. Why do you want to arrest him? He is just a child. Give me the child. I will move away from here. Just give him to me.' I tried to speak up but I was choking and only a whisper came out.

"The soldiers wanted to arrest me, but the officer in charge decided not to. I don't know why. My son, who is only six, saw a video of me on television when they were choking me. It made him so frightened.

"Things like this happen every day. If you are Israeli, you can say whatever you want without repercussions. But us, they attack us for nothing. This all happened right outside the doors of the City of David."

We asked Nihad and Jawad who else we should talk to about what is happening to Palestinian houses in Silwan. Jawad said, "Why don't you talk to Abu Ala'a and his family? Like most of us here in Silwan, their family has lost houses and gone through house demolitions."[14] Nihad called Abu Ala'a and he invited us over the following afternoon.

That night when we arrived at our guesthouse, there was a surprise waiting for us: By some miracle, our suitcases had been found and made their way to our room! We were excited to finally change our clothes.

....

14 In Palestine and other parts of the Arab world, parents are often respect-fully referred to as the father (Abu) or mother (Um) of their oldest son. Ala'a is the oldest son of Abu Ala'a and Um Ala'a.

Israelis demolishing a Palestinian house in Silwan. (Credit: Wadi Hilweh Information Center)

8
"WE'VE BEEN HERE FOR 400 YEARS": ABU ALA'A'S STORY

The next day, we met Nihad at Madaa and followed him down the stone sidewalk through the neighborhood. We stopped at a small store with stone walls and a metal door so Nihad could buy more cigarettes. Then he led us through a narrow alleyway and up a hill. Houses were crowded on both sides. Many of the houses had new stone retaining walls, flowers in window pots, metal gates, and Israeli flags flying from the rooftops. As we passed one house set back from the alley, Nihad told us it used to belong to Abu Ala'a's uncle.

Abu Ala'a's house was at the top of the hill. As we walked through the covered entryway leading to the home, the Israeli settler who lives below Abu Ala'a's family came out to stare at us. She didn't say anything—just stared. We walked by and knocked on Abu Ala'a's door. He answered the door and led us upstairs to the cement deck in front of their house. From the deck, we could look down on the Bustan neighborhood where the little boy was arrested for trying to help his mother. The buildings were crowded against each other, blocking out the sun. We couldn't see any trees or open spaces.

"When I was a child," Nihad remembered, "we would walk in the Bustan neighborhood, it was like paradise. Everything was growing—fruits and vegetables; it was green and beautiful. You felt like you were in another world. There were no markers or

> **"The Bustan neighborhood was like paradise. Everything was growing—fruits and vegetables; it was green and beautiful."**

fences, but everyone knew which plot of land was theirs, and all the families from the village grew their own food to eat and, often, to sell."

Soon Um Ala'a came out to join us with their youngest daughters: Sara, who was fourteen, and Lena, who was eight. Abu Ala'a and Um Ala'a have seven children, but the four oldest are married and live on their own. Their son Ali and his wife live with them. Sara was carrying Ali's baby; everyone took turns playing with him.

We asked Abu Ala'a to explain how his family fought to keep their home. But, like many people in Silwan, first he wanted us to understand his family's history there:

"Bismallah,[15] our family has been here for at least 400 years. Before 1948, my family had four houses in Silwan. The house that Nihad showed you on the way here was stolen from my uncle. But before my uncle, my grandfather owned the house. It was a free guesthouse. There was only one road in those days, so travelers going to al-Aqsa mosque in the Old City or east to Jordan, they all had to pass this house. My grandfather gave them food, water, everything. 'Take a rest here,' he'd say. And then they'd continue on their way.

"In 1988, Israeli settlers occupied the first houses in Silwan. They started with a house that belonged to a Palestinian family named Abbasi, but no one was living there at the time. So they moved in and took it over.

"My uncle's land was next to the Abbasi house. The next year, the settlers put up a fence inside my uncle's property and said that the land belonged to them. My uncle was a contractor

....

15   Bismallah means "in the name of Allah." In Islam, saying "bismallah" brings blessings to the beginning of an activity, including telling an important story.

and a builder. The fence they built separated him from where he parked his car and kept his building tools and wood.

"Then they tried to force their way into my uncle's house. They beat him up using electric shocks. He was an old man. My sister and my cousin were also injured."

"I don't understand," I said. "How could they do that?"

Nihad explained: "The leader of the settlers in Silwan is a man named David Be'eri. He is the head of Elad, the development corporation behind the City of David. Be'eri used to work with the Israeli Army as a leader of the special unit called the *mustarivim*. These special forces pretend they are Arabs, so Be'eri speaks Arabic very well. After he retired from the army, he came here and said he was a tourist guide.

"You know, we Palestinians are generous people. We always welcome guests. So Be'eri developed relationships with people and he started to get information about the neighborhoods in Silwan. He figured out how to use the Absentee Property Law[16] and other loopholes to steal the Abbasi house and many others. He's the one who led the attacks on Abu Ala'a's uncle and his whole family."

"How can they steal people's houses? How does that happen?" I asked.

"If Be'eri and the other settlers find a place that's empty, they try to move in," Nihad said. "If the owner comes to defend his land, maybe he will be able to keep them out or maybe not. If the settlers succeed, if they get inside, it's done. With papers of ownership, without papers, it doesn't matter. For example, behind us, do you see that house with the Israeli flags? There was

....

16   Israel's absentee property laws were originally written to legitimize Israelis moving into the homes of Palestinians forced out in 1948. More recently, they are being used to legitimize the theft by Israeli settlers of Palestinian homes and lands in East Jerusalem. You can find more information about the absentee property laws on the website of Adalah, the Legal Center for Arab Minority Rights in Israel: www.adalah.org.

a Palestinian man who lived there. But they said nobody lived there. So now they control it. They have connections in all the Israeli departments, so it's easy for them to get what they want.

"They tried to do that with Abu Ala'a's uncle. They came onto the land. They thought that nobody would say anything. But the whole family defended the land. They took on the settlers, the policemen, the soldiers. Abu Ala'a's sister and three of his cousins spent time in jail for trying to defend that land. His uncle had papers proving he owned the land. The police saw the papers, but they protected the settlers.

"The settlers have their own army, their own budget, their own rules. They didn't come here like normal strangers. They came with protection from the police, the municipal government, and the courts. So we are fighting against the state, not against ordinary people trying to steal something that is not theirs. It's not a fair war."

Abu Ala'a picked up the story: "My uncle's wife was so afraid, she had a breakdown. After a year, she died. To see something happening like this, to have these settlers try to steal her home, it affected her deep, deep, deep down.

"Meanwhile, the settlers kept attacking my uncle, trying to get his land. The second time he was beaten with cattle prods, he was hurt so badly that the ambulance had to come. The last time the police came and took my uncle away.

"We all believe my uncle died because of the electric shock from the cattle prods. The police didn't arrest Be'eri or anyone else for the attack on my uncle. We lost my uncle and my aunt to their violence. And the settlers ended up with my uncle's house and land."

By now it was late, so we had to go. We knew there was a lot more to the story and we wanted to hear Sara and Um Ala'a's stories, so we arranged to come back the next day. Nihad said he could come, too, to translate.

9
"IT'S HARD TO BE A YOUNG WOMAN HERE": SARA'S STORY

This time Ali met us at the door and introduced himself. He invited us up the stairs, past the terrace, and into the house. We sat in the living room on long, overstuffed sofas. Um Ala'a brought in little glasses of fresh-squeezed orange juice on a silver tray and placed it on the low coffee table in front of us. As Sara played with Ali's baby, Lena bounced around, making friends with Ericka, eager to be part of the conversation.

We asked Sara to tell us about her life as a teenager in Silwan.

"I am fourteen years old," Sara began, settling the baby on her lap. "What can I say? I go to school. I do activities with my friends, I come home and do my homework. If my mother needs help, I help her. I play with my brothers and sisters.

"My favorite subjects at school are Arabic and English. I love reading and writing. I am in a special writing class after school with lots of my friends. I love debka[17] and other kinds of dancing, too. Once I start dancing, I go crazy. I lose my mind."

"What's your first memory of the settlers?" I asked.

"The day when they demolished our home," she said.

"Tell us about it."

"I was little at that time—eight years old. They were standing in front of the door of our home. I went to see, but the house was

....
17 Debka is traditional Palestinian dancing.

Sara (Credit: Abu Ala'a family)

surrounded by police and their dogs. I asked my older sister what was going on. She told me to stop talking. I asked her why. 'They have come to bulldoze our house,' she said. 'If you don't stop talking, they will hit you.'

"They locked us in a room downstairs, and we could hear them tearing our house apart over our heads."

"Did they give you a reason?" I asked.

"We were adding onto the house without a building permit. If you are Palestinian, they will not give you a permit, even to add on one room. Then if you do it anyway, they use it as an excuse to demolish your whole house. That's what happened to us."

"How did the situation affect you?" Nihad asked.

"Afterwards, I kept dreaming the same nightmare about what happened that day. Sometimes I still see it in my dreams. For a long time, I felt afraid. But I am not afraid anymore."

Nihad said: "I need to tell you what it is like for girls like Sara. There are settlers living all around this family, and they watch everything. You saw as we knocked at the door, they stop everything to stare at us like we are strangers and they have the right.

"If Sara wants to go to al-Aqsa mosque or the market, she has to pass through the Jewish quarter of the Old City. Almost everyone living there now is Jewish—this is very different from the situation only a few years ago. When Sara tries to walk by, they swear at her, they say bad words. Sometimes they hit her. This happens not only with Sara, this happens with her mother, with many, many women and girls. And these are big groups of boys, not just one or two. These groups of Jewish boys attack Palestinian boys who must pass through the neighborhood, too. So they face this problem nearly every day because there is no choice, they have to pass through that area to get to the mosque, to the market. If Sara turns around and goes another way, through another gate into the Old City, it will take her much longer. And even if you find a route where there are no settlers, there are soldiers and policemen. If you escape from the fire, you will drown in the water."

Sara nodded. "It's hard to be a young woman here. Because the settlers are trying to take over al-Aqsa Mosque, we women and girls have been demonstrating—occupying the mosque to keep it safe. When the settlers and the soldiers barge in, we chant 'God is great.' This is not violence or terrorist words. It's part of our religion. But one of the women soldiers hit me, and one of the men threw a noise bomb right at my leg.

"This makes me scared and nervous. Every day while going to the mosque, I have to pass by many settlers and I know that I might not get back home. I might be beaten, I might face a hundred fates.

"My school is in a different neighborhood in Silwan. Sometimes it's difficult to get there, and sometimes not. One day recently the settlers took over a house near us. I was leaving for school when the Israeli army surrounded the area. I told them that

"We have the determination to struggle and we have the patience for it. We believe that we will get our rights back."

I just wanted to go to school, but they said that no one was allowed to move. I told them: 'I don't want to be late for school! I have an exam. It is 7:30 already.'

"'No!' they yelled at me. 'You are not allowed to go.' Because I told them I needed to get through, they threw noise bombs and tear gas at us. One of the soldiers even hit me in the face with his stick and shouted, 'Get away from here.' They wouldn't let anyone out to go to work or school."

"What is it like at school?" I asked. "Do the teachers support you?"

"We want to know about our history. Sometimes we do it with our teacher secretly; talking about Palestinian history is forbidden because our school is run by the Israeli Jerusalem Municipality. The teachers are supposed to give the students the education that the municipality wants—the history of Israel, not the history of Palestine. So our history teacher tries to mention that there is Palestine, but the history I know, really I learned it at Madaa and from my father."

Nihad added: "This is the thing about Israel. They think they are so smart when they want Sara's generation to grow up in fear. They think they will stop them from thinking about the situation, that they will feel inferior and they will not do anything. But they are creating the opposite response. The young people are growing up surrounded by hatred, and that makes them think: 'Why are they acting like this? We have to search and find out why.' So the Israelis are pushing this generation of Palestinians to study our history."

"Is there anything else you want us to tell teenagers in the United States?" Ericka asked.

"We Palestinians are patient," Sara said. "We know God is

with us, whatever happens. Even if it hurts, we have to stay determined and strong to fight the enemy who wants to take our country and wants to do wrong to us. We believe that God will be fair with us—make it possible for us to find justice. We have the determination to struggle and we have the patience for it. We believe that we will get our rights back. What they are doing to us—the occupation—doesn't make us weak, it makes us stronger. They try to take our rights, but we believe that God will bring us back our rights."

10

"THEY DEMOLISHED OUR HOUSE!": UM ALA'A'S STORY

Um Ala'a brought in a coffee pot and little white cups on matching plates. The coffee was strong, thick, and sweet, flavored with cardamom pods.

"Please," I said as she passed out the cups, "tell us about your life."

"I was born here in Silwan, my whole life is here. When I was a child and even a teenager, the situation was much better. Even though we were under occupation, we used to have fun. The repression wasn't so intense. As Jerusalemites, we used to be able to take a car and go to the West Bank, Nablus, or Jaffa without anybody stopping us to demand, 'I need to see your ID.' Now, not just to move from city to city, but between neighborhoods, you have to go through a checkpoint. Now, here in my neighborhood, in front of my house, the police come to ask me, 'What are you doing here?' This is all to protect the settlers. The settlers have ruined our life.

"Sara told you about when our house was demolished. But I want to tell you from the perspective of a mother. Our son Ali was of marriageable age and we wanted to help him get married. The settlers have taken so many houses, rentals are very, very expensive and hard to find. We wanted to help him build a place to live, so we decided to add a floor on top of our house for him.

"The settlers saw that we were building an addition to our house, so they informed on us to the Jerusalem Municipality. The municipality won't give permission for Palestinians to build—only Israelis. So if you are Palestinian and you need somewhere to put your family, you have to build without a permit. You have no choice.

"Early one morning, the Israeli forces came and completely surrounded the area. They had workers and a bulldozer. They pounded on the door: 'We are going to demolish the house!'

"My children and I were sleeping. They were young—Sara was eight and Lena was only two. My elderly uncle was here as well. He was visiting from Jordan. Abu Ala'a and my sons were at work. Imagine that you are sleeping and wake up to see this at the door of your house. They brought a dog into the house. 'Get the dog out,' I said. 'You will scare my kids.'

"I tried to get out of the house to see what was happening, but they didn't let me. They grabbed my hands and forced me back in. They were yelling at me in Hebrew.

"I told them I don't speak Hebrew. One of them told me in Arabic, 'You have to stay here. We are going to demolish your house.'

"I called Abu Ala'a and my son Ala'a. They came right away. After an argument outside, they allowed Abu Ala'a to enter but didn't allow my son Ala'a. They made him stay at the bottom of the street. And they destroyed all our hard work.

"After that, it took us two years to rebuild the house. My son was supposed to get married that summer, but we had to delay the wedding for a year. You know, we have a traditional way to marry; it's not like Western cultures. Our sons tend to marry early—when they are twenty or twenty-two. Even twenty-six is late. But now, there are no places to live, so they don't marry until late—thirty or even later."

"What is it like to be a mother in these circumstances?" I asked.

"We live under occupation. No matter what a mother does to protect her children, she can't control the situation. I worry the most when one of them is not at home. If Ali is late getting home at night, I start to worry: What happened to him? Did they arrest him? Did the settlers shoot him? Did they beat him? I am worried all the time. This kills you slowly.

"A few years ago, when Ali was in his early twenties, there were clashes in Silwan and the police didn't want our youth to go anywhere, or even leave the house. Ali was at his uncle's home, just next door. When he left his uncle's house to come home, the soldiers stopped him and asked for his ID. He said, 'My ID is in my house. I just went next door to my uncle's house.'

> **"Our young women have no choice but to defend themselves. Young men have been brave, but nowadays young women are braver."**

"They started to beat him. Somebody called Abu Ala'a and told him, 'Hurry, your son is being beaten by the soldiers.' There were seven soldiers beating Ali. He showed them how close the houses were, but they didn't give him any chance to go home and get his ID. They beat him and teargassed him, right in front of his home. I saw that with my own eyes.

"Before, the settlers didn't bother the girls. We used to be more afraid for the boys than the girls. Now there is no difference; maybe the experience of the young girls is worse. The soldiers and the settlers don't mind beating, arresting, or abusing young women. So our young women have no choice but to defend themselves. Young men have been brave, but nowadays young women are braver.

"Sometimes when we see how the whole world is behaving toward us as Palestinians, it feels useless to say anything. Here we are in the twenty-first century, and there are still people under occupation.

"In the face of all this, we do what we can. Here we are lucky to have the Madaa Center. It helps the children. They teach them

As we walked through the Old City and the streets of Silwan, we seesawed between working in solidarity with Palestinians living under occupation and reaping the privileges of looking like Jewish settlers.

debka and music. They do their best to help children forget the settlers, and to change their miserable life through different activities. It is a lovely place for the kids to breathe. To have fun. It gives them a chance to see that life is not just settlers and the occupation. We don't want the kids to be sitting all the time, watching killings and horrible things on TV. We want them, for a little bit, to be far away from these things, to live their childhood."

By now, I could see the sun setting through the windows. I knew Nihad wanted to get back to his family, so I said we needed to go. But Um Ala'a and Abu Ala'a wouldn't let us go. Abu Ala'a told us to sit back down, and Um Ala'a brought out a large platter of tiny eggplants, stuffed with rice and meat and stewed in a tomato sauce with olives. Lena passed out plates, Abu Ala'a gave everyone too many eggplants, and we ate around the low coffee table. It was delicious. Then Um Ala'a brought tangerines that she peeled and broke into sections, fresh almonds that we ate by dipping them in sugar for each bite, and strawberries. Then more coffee.

After thanking the family, we walked with Nihad through the alley and up the hill toward the Old City. We stopped at Nihad's house, across the street from Madaa and a few houses down from the excavation site at the corner. He took us around the back of the house to show us the cracks in the foundation caused by the tunneling underneath. He told us he couldn't figure out how to stop his house from leaking during the winter rains. Ericka took pictures of the cracked walls, then we said thank you and good night.

Across the street at the Madaa Center, the teachers were trying to shoo the children out the door and home for dinner. Just a few steps further up the hill, guards with Uzi machine guns guarded the entrance to the City of David. Turning left at the corner, we threaded our way through crowds of tourists getting onto buses and into taxis. They poured out of the Mughrabi Gate as we tried to make our way inside. To get back to the Lutheran Guesthouse, we had to walk up the narrow, stone-paved Jewish Quarter Road past settlers' houses and newly consecrated synagogues.

This was the same road that Sara and her brothers walked to get to school and the mosque; this was the same road where they were threatened daily. But no one paid any attention to us; we fit seamlessly into the scenery.

This was the craziest part of being in East Jerusalem. As we walked through the Old City and the streets of Silwan, we seesawed between working in solidarity with Palestinians living under occupation and reaping the privileges of looking like Jewish settlers. As soon as we weren't with Nihad, the settlers accepted us as their own. No one ever hassled us in the Old City. Young settlers politely shared the path; security guards told us where to go when we were lost. Although I have lived in the United States my whole life, much of it spent teaching about and fighting racism, I have never had such a visceral experience of white privilege as in the streets of Palestine.

II

THE CITY OF DAVID: ARCHEOLOGY AS A WEAPON

That night, Ericka and I talked about taking a tour at the City of David National Park. We were nervous; we hoped none of the guards would recognize us as people who were going to Madaa every day. And going on the tour felt disloyal to our Palestinian friends—this was a place they were forbidden to enter. The construction there was destroying their neighborhood and erasing their history.

But how the City of David uses archeology as a weapon is a critical piece of the story of Silwan. We wanted to see the excavation first-hand and hear what they were telling tourists. We decided to go. I would try to record as much as I could with a tape recorder concealed in my pocket; Ericka would take photos like any other tourist.

By then, it was almost midnight, but I pulled up the City of David website on my computer and tried to navigate the options. We could play paint ball, take a ropes course, or hold a birthday party. We could book a tour in German, French, Spanish, Arabic, Hebrew, or English. I signed us up for what I thought was a basic tour in English and entered my credit card information.

"This is way too expensive," I complained when the receipt popped up. Ericka, who was half asleep, came over to see what the problem was.

"You signed us up for the segway tour!" The image of us segwaying our way through the City of David, Ericka trying to take photos and me trying to take notes—without falling off our scooters—was too much. The tension from trying to stay focused in the face of what we were seeing and hearing made us both giddy. We collapsed in hysterical laughter, only a step from tears.

The next morning, I explained my mistake to someone on the phone, she changed our tickets, and we set off for the basic walking tour.

As Jawad and Nihad had explained, the City of David National Park is the cornerstone of the Elad development organization. Elad was founded in 1986 by David Be'eri—the man who led the attack on Abu Ala'a's uncle. The City of David is the only national park that is run by a private corporation instead of the state of Israel. Recently, it's also called Jerusalem Walls National Park, laying out a stake to all of the Old City and the areas surrounding it.

Passing the guards at the entrance, we walked through the stone gate, just like any other Jewish tourists from the United States. Once inside, we looked at the display map built into a large table in the center of the courtyard. The big hole across the street from the park was labeled the Givati Parking Lot. The map showed the tunnels under Silwan, and we could see that one of them ran right under Nihad's house. We climbed up a tower with views of the entire Silwan Valley. English, Hebrew, Chinese, and French conversations overlapped as visitors browsed the museum store, posed for photographs, and bought snacks as they waited for their tours to start.

Ericka pointed out what goes unnoticed by most of the tourists here—two homes above the plaza, behind barbed wire, that have been completely cut off from their neighborhood. They were easily recognizable as Palestinian by the black water tanks on the roof. There was laundry hanging on a string line out the window, and a children's push toy abandoned by the fence.

We wandered around the plaza, peeking into the birthday room, where the table was set with paper plates, streamers, and favors for a party later in the day.

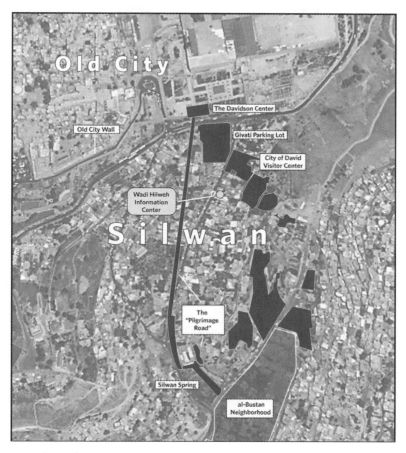

City of David excavations, tourist areas, and planned tourist areas in the Wadi Hilweh neighborhood of Silwan. The black areas on the map are already part of the City of David. They plan to make the entire al-Bustan neighborhood (shaded gray) an Israeli park.(Credit: Emek Shaveh/Henry Bortman)

When we told Nihad we were going to the City of David, he had described what the plaza used to look like: "Before the visitors center was built, an elderly couple from the Shahada-Qareen family lived here and cultivated fruit trees. The entire area was an orchard and they made their living selling the fruit to the villagers. My family bought fruit from them. Most of all I remember the woman, who lived for several years after her husband died.

After her death, the land was transferred to the settlers, probably through the absentee property laws. At the entrance to the orchard, there was a very large eucalyptus tree. The tree was a beautiful source of shade on hot summer days, but most of all it was a meeting place. When you made a date at the tree, everyone knew it meant that large eucalyptus tree. Today, the guard post sits on the spot where the tree was."

Soon it was time for our tour to begin. Rebecca, our tour leader, was enthusiastic and full of information, working hard to keep the children interested and to bridge the gap between the US, Australian, and Israeli tourists. She told us she was born in the United States and moved to Israel in her teens. First she volunteered at the City of David, and then became part of the educational staff.

"Where was David from?" Rebecca asked us after we walked down wooden stairs to an excavated section beneath the plaza.

"He was born in Bethlehem," she told us when no one responded, "but he was from Hebron, which is south of us. And Saul [who, according to the Bible, was king before David] was from the tribe of Benjamin, north of us. So when David wanted to unite all Jews, he picked Jerusalem, a place halfway in between. It didn't belong to anyone, so it belonged to everyone. That's true today. Jerusalem belongs to all the people of Israel.

"How do we know that this is where David's castle was? According to the Bible, King David's palace is the highest point in Jerusalem. This is the highest point in Jerusalem, so it has to be King David's palace."

She explained to us that archeologists have been digging in Silwan since the nineteenth century, and she described additional "proof" that we were on the site of David's palace: Archeologists at the site discovered two impressions from official seals. Back before driver's licenses and birth certificates, wealthy people and their assistants stamped documents with personalized etched or carved seals to prove they were legitimate. The "King David" seals were marked with the names of two men who were mentioned in the Bible (Jeremiah 37:3, 38:1) as officials of King Zedekiah.

"Isn't that amazing?" she asked us. "Now we have concrete proof that this was King David's palace."

Ericka and I looked at each other. What kind of proof was that? The seals don't say anything about King David or where his palace was located. There is actually disagreement among archeologists about whether David was a real person, but even if we take the Bible as evidence that he was, he lived during the tenth century BCE. Zedekiah ruled in the sixth century BCE—400 years later.

But we were on the tour to collect information, not argue, so we didn't say anything. Rebecca showed us a stepped stone structure that she said dated to the tenth century BCE and said it was one of the support walls for David's palace. (We read later in a report by Emek Shaveh, an Israeli organization that advocates for responsible archeology, that there are remains of a number of buildings in the area that date to the tenth century BCE, but nothing that connects them specifically to David.)[18]

Then Rebecca took us across the street to the Givati Parking Lot. She led us through a gate into the fenced excavation area. It was much larger than we realized from the street. A well-built wooden walkway surrounded the site, which dropped more than two stories below street level. Tarps were strung up at various intervals where tourists and volunteer excavators could find shade.

Rebecca led us down the wooden stairs and assembled us on a platform near the bottom of the excavation. She showed us a horizontal tunnel that Elad excavators dug parallel to Wadi Hilweh Street. It was the tunnel we saw on the map in the plaza, and it was clear that it ran right under Nihad's house. No wonder the walls were cracking! Ericka took a picture to show him later.

....

18   Emek Shaveh. *Archeology in the Shadow of the Conflict: The Mound of Ancient Jerusalem in Silwan.* 10 September 2013. 10 September 2020 < alt-arch.org/en/booklet_online/>.

"We're not supposed to tunnel in the other direction, under the Old City toward the Temple Mount, but we're doing it anyway."

Rebecca said that Elad hoped to turn the tunnel into a stairway that tourists could climb all the way from the Silwan Spring (which she called Siloam Spring) up to the Western Wall. She said that this "stepped street" was the path that Jews took in ancient times, washing themselves in the spring, then hiking up to the Temple Mount in the Old City. "Of course," she said, "politically it's very, very difficult to excavate here."

"Why?" a woman behind us asked her friend.

"Because there are people—Palestinians—living in all those houses," her friend responded.

Rebecca didn't hear her. "Don't worry," she said in a theatrical whisper. "We're not supposed to tunnel in the other direction, under the Old City toward the Temple Mount, but we're doing it anyway."

This was the only time on our tour that anyone mentioned that Palestinians live in Silwan, or that hundreds have been displaced by the excavations and the incoming Israeli settlers. Because of the way the City of David is constructed, especially the extensive systems of tunnels, the hundreds of thousands of tourists who come to the park never see a Palestinian, and never realize what impact the park has had on their lives and future. They never learn that the excavations caused a classroom to fall into the tunnels or about the houses that have been damaged. They never learn that the cultural café was demolished, or that the Givati Parking Lot used to be a Palestinian marketplace, a soccer field, and the site of many wedding parties.

Rebecca led us through the tunnel—not in the direction of Nihad's house, but the other way, under the street, under the Mughrabi Gate, into the Old City. We came up in the Davidson Archeological Park, near the Western Wall. Davidson is one of a series of recent Israeli archeological exhibits and excavation sites in the Old City. The tunnel links Israel's plans to take over Silwan with their plans to take over the Old City.

Rebecca was finishing up our tour, but my mind was wandering. I was thinking about archeology. I always thought of it as a science, exhibits in a museum that showed interesting things about ancient civilizations. But here in Jerusalem it was a colonial weapon—telling a "single story" that tried to make it OK to take over people's land and history, and even their future.

In Jerusalem archeology is a colonial weapon— telling a "single story" that tries to make it OK to take over people's land and history, and even their future.

Over and over again, Rebecca equated stories from the Bible and archeological evidence. Sometimes she mentioned one, sometimes the other, as if both were historical facts. For example, when she told us that the Bible says that David's palace is at the highest point in Jerusalem, and the City of David Park is the highest point in Jerusalem—that's interesting, but it's not archeological evidence. Archeological evidence is artifacts that are carefully collected, mapped, dated, compared with other evidence, and evaluated by many different archeologists in the course of developing a theory about their meaning.

That night, Ericka and I used the internet to explore what biblical archeologists (archeologists who study civilizations and events mentioned in the Bible) say about the relationship between the Bible and archeology. According to one of those experts, William Dever, professor emeritus at the University of Arizona:

> From the beginnings of what we call biblical archeology, perhaps 150 years ago, scholars, mostly western scholars, have attempted to use archeological data to prove the Bible. And for a long time it was thought to work. William Foxwell

Albright, the great father of our discipline, often spoke of the "archeological revolution." Well, the revolution has come but not in the way that Albright thought. The truth of the matter today is that archeology raises more questions about the historicity of the Hebrew Bible and even the New Testament than it provides answers, and that's very disturbing to some people.

But perhaps we were asking the wrong questions . . . We want to make the Bible history. Many people think it has to be history or nothing. But there is no word for history in the Hebrew Bible. In other words, what did the biblical writers think they were doing? Writing objective history? No. That's a modern discipline. They were telling stories . . .

I have always thought that if we resurrected someone from the past, one of the biblical writers, they would be amused, because for them it would have made no difference. I think they would have said, faith is faith is faith—take your proofs and go with them.[19]

In other words, they were trying to make a religious point, not an historical one.

Rebecca didn't merge the Bible and archeology on her own: that approach seems to underlie everything that Elad does. The first page of *Discovering the City of David: A Journey to the Source*, the official guidebook to the park, says: "About 3,000 years ago young King David conquered the city from the Jebusites and made it his royal capital, thus forging the eternal bond between the nation of Israel and Jerusalem."

"The eternal bond between the nation of Israel and Jerusalem"—that is the real purpose of the City of David. To make the case that all of Jerusalem belongs to Israel, and that the

....

19   Glassman, Gary. Interview with William Dever. "Archeology of the Hebrew Bible," The Bible's Hidden Secrets Series, *Nova* July 2007. 10 September 2020 <www.pbs.org/wgbh/nova/bible/dever.html>.

Palestinians who live in Silwan and throughout East Jerusalem are intruders.

Many, many cultures have left their mark on Silwan. Fascinating remains of all of those cultures have been found in Silwan and the Old City, but Rebecca only talked about artifacts that connected the past to the current nation of Israel. As Nassar Ibrahim, from the Alternative Information Center in the al-Bustan neighborhood of Silwan, wrote: "[For the Israelis] there is no room for Canaanite, Palestinian, Phoenician, Egyptian, Roman, Greek, Arab, Muslim, and Christian names . . . There is room for only a single narrative."[20]

According to Emek Shaveh, what has happened at the Givati Parking Lot is a good example.[21] Elad's plan for the lot is to build a tourist destination called the Kedem Center, a massive seven-story building. As soon as they started excavating, it was clear that the area was filled with extraordinary artifacts from many eras. If archeology were the priority, archeologists would have marked the area off into sections, then carefully sifted through layer after layer, making careful maps of what was found where and labeling the discoveries for later analysis.

But the priority was making the lot available for construction, and discovering artifacts only about the Jewish past. So they excavated quickly to reach the earliest layers.

In order to do that, the developers reinforced the excavation pit with concrete poured into shafts bored down from the surface into bedrock far below, destroying artifacts along the way. Then, a cemetery, probably from the eleventh century CE, was removed from the site—100 boxes of human bones. Experts believe these

....

20   Ibrahim, Nassar. "The Bustan in Silwan: Al-Quds Will Live on Forever and Resist in Its Own Way," *Al Bustan in Silwan.* Alternative Information Center, 2012.

21   Emek Shaveh. *"Beit Haliba" and the Givati Parking Lot Archeological Excavations and Their Effect on the Status Quo in the Old City of Jerusalem and in Silwan,* 9 September 2013. 10 September 2020 <www.alt-arch.org/en/haliba/>.

How did the conflict between Palestinians and Israelis get to this terrible point?

were from the Fatimid or Mamluk periods, about which very little is known. The excavators also removed many Islamic period remains, including a residential area with houses and a street, the entire Byzantine layer, and the Roman layer. What could have been learned from all those archeological treasures is lost forever.

It had been an upsetting day. There we were, part of a group of tourists listening to a story that justified the tunnels, that made destroying Silwan seem like an obviously good thing, and that completely ignored the Palestinians we had been getting to know and care about—as if they didn't even exist.

How did the conflict between Palestinians and Israelis get to this terrible point? Ericka and I knew that learning more about the history, especially the recent history of Silwan and the Old City, was the next step.

12
IT DIDN'T START WITH THE HOLOCAUST

My high school students were often recent immigrants to the United States. In the beginning of the year, I would ask them to write about culture shock. "What surprised you the most? What was the hardest thing to understand about life in the United States?" I asked. The most common answer was racism. They were confused and scared by the level of tension, especially between white people and Black people, and why people in the United States see everything in terms of race. After we studied US history—from what happened to Native Americans when the Europeans arrived and started to steal their land, to slavery, to segregation, to the police killings of Black and Brown youth now—it started to make sense. You have to know the history to understand the present.

The same is true for Palestine and Israel. Most US history textbooks say that Jews settled Israel during and after World War II, fleeing the Holocaust, Nazi Germany's efforts to exterminate Jewish people and culture. But the story of modern-day Israel actually started many years earlier, toward the end of the nineteenth century.

For hundreds of years, Jews lived in many countries in Europe, including Russia, Germany, Poland, and France. Jews also lived in North Africa and the Middle East. Often they were mistreated. In Russia and Eastern Europe, for example, they had to live in special neighborhoods called ghettos, and were often attacked.

In some countries they weren't allowed to go to college or own land. Discrimination against Jews is called anti-semitism.

Jews responded in various ways to anti-semitism. Some people emigrated to the Americas. Others joined revolutions in their home countries, hoping that the new government would be better for everyone.

One group of Jews, led by Theodor Herzl, decided that Jews needed their own country. They called themselves Zionists. The Zionists had an international meeting in 1897 and decided that they wanted to move to Palestine and make it their country. They thought about a few different places—including Uganda and Argentina—but decided on Palestine. At that time, there were about 246,300 Muslims, 24,000 Jews, and 21,800 Christians living in Palestine. They all thought of themselves as Palestinians.

In the early twentieth century, Zionist Jews started to move to Palestine a few at a time. At that point, the Zionist settlers were buying land, not stealing it, and relationships with the Palestinians were often friendly. Most Palestinians were farmers, but there were cities, too. Bethlehem and Jerusalem were cities that many people from around the world came to visit because they are important cities in the Bible and the Quran.[22]

Palestine was colonized by many different empires over the centuries, but usually the lives of everyday people didn't change much. When Zionist settlers first came to Palestine, the country was ruled by the Ottoman Empire, which controlled most of the Middle East in those days. Then World War I happened. On one side were the Allies: England, France, Russia, and eventually the United States. On the other side were the Central Powers: Germany, Austria-Hungary, Bulgaria, and the Ottoman Empire. To help them win the war, the Allies promised independence to the Arab peoples who had been colonized by the Ottoman Empire if they joined the Allies' side. But the Europeans double-crossed

....

22   The Quran (or Koran) is the sacred book of Islam.

the Arab resistance fighters: France and England met secretly and divided up the Middle East between themselves. France took colonial control of Syria, Lebanon, and southern Turkey. England took what is now Iraq, Kuwait, Jordan, and Palestine. That treaty, signed in 1916, is called the Sykes-Picot Agreement.

Meanwhile, the Zionists were pressuring England to give Palestine to them. Arthur Balfour, England's foreign secretary, agreed. He wrote a letter to Zionist leader Baron Rothschild in 1917 that said, "His majesty's government view[s] with favor the establishment in Palestine of a national home for the Jewish people, and will use their best endeavors to facilitate the achievement of this project." That letter is known as the Balfour Declaration.

When the Palestinians found out about these agreements, they held a conference to figure out what to do next.

"Wait!" they said. "You can't make Palestine a Zionist country. It isn't empty. We live here. You promised us independence. We want to be our own country." England didn't listen. The Palestinians organized the Great Revolt, a general strike and a rebellion that lasted from 1936 to 1939, demanding independence and an end to colonial rule, but they didn't succeed in forcing England to leave.

More and more Zionist settlers were coming to Palestine, particularly as Nazi Germany began killing and imprisoning more and more Jews. By the end of World War II, six million Jews had been murdered by the Nazis. But instead of the creation of a safe place for Jews in Germany, the country responsible for the Holocaust, the war resulted in an enormous increase in Jewish immigration to Palestine and international support for the establishment of the Jewish state of Israel there. The United States, like many other countries, didn't want to open their doors to "too many" Jewish refugees, so they encouraged survivors of the war to go to Palestine instead.

England decided to leave Palestine in 1947. They proposed that the newly formed United Nations split Palestine into two countries: Israel and Palestine.

During the Nakba, more than 750,000 Palestinians were forced out of their homes and off their lands. (Credit: UNRWA Archives)

The Palestinians said, "No. This is our country. You can't divide it and give more than half of it to someone else."

Despite Palestinian protests, the United Nations agreed to partition Palestine—giving more than half, with almost all of the access to the Mediterranean and arable land, to the Zionists. A smaller piece, divided into sections, was supposed to go to the Palestinians. And the city of Jerusalem—important to Muslims, Christians, and Jews for religious reasons—was designated an international city under the jurisdiction of the United Nations.

The Palestinians were upset about how unfair that plan was. They couldn't even imagine how much worse things would become.

By the end of World War II in 1945, the Zionists had lots of weapons. They had been preparing for many years, trained and armed by the British. Starting in the 1930s, they mapped every village in Palestine—roads, houses, schools, and other public buildings; water sources; the best hills for defense; which villagers had participated in the 1936 revolt. On the other hand, during the years when Palestine was under British control, it was illegal for Palestinians to have a gun. You could be imprisoned or killed if you were caught with a weapon. So the Palestinians were ill-prepared to defend themselves.

Palestinians had a country and then, suddenly, they didn't.

Zionist attacks on Palestinians increased dramatically in 1947 as the British began to withdraw from Palestine. Beginning that fall and escalating in 1948, the Zionists began a well-planned strategy to kill, terrorize, and uproot the Palestinian population.[23] Within a few months, 750,000 Palestinians were forced into exile. Palestinians had a country and then, suddenly, they didn't.

Israel declared itself a Jewish state on May 15, 1948. Israelis celebrate that date as Independence Day. Palestinians commemorate the same date as *al-Nakba*—Arabic for "the catastrophe."

....
23   Pappé, Ilan. *The Ethnic Cleansing of Palestine*. OneWorld. 2006.

Yacoub Odeh above the ruins of Lifta, his village. (Credit: Vinciane Jacquet)

13

"AFTER THEY KICKED US OUT, THEY BLEW UP OUR VILLAGE": YACOUB'S STORY

Ericka and I knew the basic history of the Nakba, but we wanted to know what happened in the Silwan area, and what it felt like to live through that period. Ericka needed to make plans for her return to the United States, so I made an appointment to talk with Yacoub Odeh, who had been a young boy living in a village very close to Silwan in 1948. He asked me to meet him at the Jerusalem Hotel, a famous old hotel on the north side of the Old City. Sahar told me to stand on Wadi Hilweh Street near the little store and take the bus around the Old City to the Damascus Gate. From there I could walk to the hotel.

A white shuttle bus came by, but I wasn't sure whether it was Israeli or Palestinian, so I let it go. After twenty minutes, a big blue bus clunked and smoked its way up the hill. I could see the Palestinian flag in the window, so I waved to the bus driver to stop and let me in. The front of the bus was hung with dozens of stuffed animals and Palestinian banners. It reminded me of buses in Mexico because the driver had made the inside his own. An elderly man with a beard and a long traditional Palestinian robe pointed me to a seat. We went around the eastern side of the Old City. We passed a cemetery and a sign that said "Jericho Road." It reminded me of the story of Jericho in the Bible. I wondered how old that road was. How many hundreds of years had people used it to travel from Jerusalem to Jericho?

The bus stopped at Herod's Gate and many people got off. At the next stop, I hesitated. It didn't seem like we were quite at the Damascus Gate. But a young Palestinian woman who was getting off the bus motioned to me to get off, too. She must have heard me tell the bus driver that I was looking for Damascus Gate. I was amazed that both she and the old man would go out of their way to be helpful to someone who looked like a settler.

I was early, so I sat and drank tea in the hotel bar until Yacoub arrived. It was like visiting the old British colonial occupation of Palestine: The tables and chairs were wicker, the chair cushions covered in chintz—shiny flowered fabric. There were hanging plants everywhere.

Amongst the European tourists in the bar, Yacoub was easy to identify when he walked in the door. A Palestinian elder with a salt-and-pepper mustache and a mostly bald head, he walked like it was painful to move. The stress of his life experiences was etched into his face, but his eyes were sharp and clear. We changed seats three times until we found somewhere quiet enough for an interview. As we got to know each other, Yacoub asked who I was working with in Silwan, and what Palestinians I knew in the United States. We realized we had friends and colleagues in common.

"Please start," I said, "with what life was like here before the Nakba."

"I am a refugee from Lifta village," he explained. "I was born in Lifta May 20, 1940. My father was a farmer and we lived close to the Lifta Spring. Our house had a veranda to the south; from there we could see everything that happened in the village. We had two floors—the living quarters were upstairs and below them were two rooms, one to store food for the family and the other for the chickens, the cows, and the donkey. This was normal in Lifta village.

"In one of my first memories, I was very young, collecting eggs from our chickens. I accidentally broke one. I also remember being with my older sister and other children from the village. We were looking for a plant that the girls crushed to get a liquid to color their nails and their hands. It wasn't henna, but it was like henna.

"I loved to play in the spring; I was like a fish. At the spring, there were two pools—one for household use, cleaning clothes and dishes, and the other for the animals. There were taps in the village for drinking water.

"I used to go to the pools and collect the water in a tin cup and dribble it on the rocks under our house to make a stream. I loved to make a muddy mess."

"What happened to Lifta during the Nakba?" I asked. I knew that Yacoub didn't have much time to talk, and I wanted to be sure we got to what I saw as the important part of our interview. But Yacoub wouldn't be rushed. He wanted to make sure I understood what Lifta was like before the Nakba.

Yacoub wouldn't be rushed. He wanted to make sure I understood what Lifta was like before the Nakba.

"It was a lovely life there," he continued. "We had beautiful gardens in the village. From the two pools, the water ran down the land into the gardens. The people of Lifta said the water was for all. They divided the land among the people who lived in the village according to how many people were in the family. One family's plot was ten meters square; a larger family got twenty meters. And everyone planted as they liked. We grew all kinds of vegetables and fruits because it wasn't too hot or too cold and there was always water. As children, we spent many hours playing in the pools and the gardens.

"Lifta is just west of Jerusalem; we called it one of Jerusalem's daughters. It's on the road between the Jaffa Gate in the Old City and the city of Jaffa, on the Mediterranean coast. Before 1948, there were more than 550 houses in our village, about 3,000 people. Lifta was designed to be very beautiful, the houses had carved entrances to the windows and the doors.

Lifta's distinctive stone craftsmanship is still evident in the shell of this house. Zionists destroyed Lifta and forced the Palestinian residents to leave in February 1948. (Credit: János Chialá)

"Lifta had an upper part and a lower part; the school was between, easy for everyone to get to. It was close to a huge olive grove. When the bell rang at the end of the day, we jumped from our desks, ran outside, and bounded from rock to rock to get to town. There was a sports festival every year at the school; I went with my parents to watch my older brother Daoud compete."

"When did you first realize that Lifta was in danger?" I asked.

"One day, toward the end of 1947, I was with my mother and small brother in front of our house. She was making a fire in the local way with wood. Suddenly Daoud ran into the yard shouting, 'Look, they are shooting!'

"My mother took us inside and told us to hide under the table in a corner. This was before Israel declared itself a state in May 1948, but there were already Zionist armed gangs that were attacking Palestinian villages. By this time, they controlled the upper part of Lifta and they were shooting at Palestinians coming back from the Old City.

"They forced the villagers living in upper Lifta out of their homes, and wouldn't let anyone go into the Old City through the Jaffa Gate. The Old City was our life center—economics, education, health, everything. People tried to travel around and enter the Old City by another gate, but then the Zionist gangs began shooting them on the bypass roads. Day after day the Zionists got stronger because the British gave them military equipment.

"My father carried my younger sister... They shot at him but he wasn't injured. On his robe, you could see the hole from the bullet that went right between his legs."

"One time the Zionists attacked a café. They killed six people and injured another seven. I remember the funeral; they brought the dead people down by our spring and then took them to the graveyard. Everyone was praying, the women were weeping and weeping. We were sitting on the veranda. I asked my mother what happened and she told me.

"Another night there was so much shooting that our parents took us to a house in the middle of the village for refuge. There were many of us crowded together and the people who lived there made a fire to keep us warm.

"In February 1948, the day came when we had to leave our house."

"That's still before Israel became a state," I said. "The British hadn't left yet, right?"

"Lifta was one of the first villages that the Zionist gangs forced the Palestinians to leave. I will tell you why: because the location was so strategic. One of the Zionist goals was the total destruction of the villages from Jaffa to the Jaffa Gate. They wanted control of that route, slicing the country in two, as part of their war plan. Lifta was one of those villages. And they succeeded. None of these villages remain.

"I still remember that terrible day. My father carried my

"We had left without packing anything because we thought in a day or two we would return."

younger sister and I followed with my older sister. My father told us to hurry. They shot at him but he wasn't injured. On his robe, you could see the hole from the bullet that went right between his legs. My mother kept that robe for many years.

"My parents found someone driving a truck. In the back there were children from three families and we were the fourth family. We escaped in the truck with my mother. My father and the other men returned to Lifta to resist the Zionists.

"First the truck was going to take us to Abu Ghosh. But it was too dangerous. Instead we went to Beitunia. We spent one or two nights in an empty house, and then our family began to live under a huge fig tree. There was a small storage shed. My mother and sisters slept inside the shed. Daoud and I slept in front under the fig tree.

"After they kicked us out of our villages, they blew them up. The military aircraft came and dropped big containers of TNT that exploded and made holes in the land. We could see the bombs falling from the planes. I remember seeing a huge hole right in front of me.

"My father and the other men stayed in Lifta until the massacre at Deir Yassin on April 9, 1948."

I knew about Deir Yassin. It had been a nearby village, just over the hill from Lifta. The village had a nonaggression pact with the Zionist militias, but the Zionists wanted to create an example that would terrify Palestinians all over the country into leaving their homes. They burst into the village without warning, spraying machine-gun fire and killing many of the residents. Then they gathered the rest of the villagers together and murdered them in cold blood.

In his book *The Ethnic Cleansing of Palestine*,[24] Israeli historian Ilan Pappé quotes Fahim Zaydan, who lived in Deir Yassin at that time. He was twelve years old: "They took us out one after the other, shot an old man and, when one of his daughters cried, she was shot, too. Then they called my brother Muhammad and shot him in front of us. When my mother yelled, bending over him—carrying my little sister Hudra in her hands, still breastfeeding her—they shot her, too."

Zaydan was shot but he survived. Altogether, ninety-three villagers were murdered, plus the resistance fighters who tried to defend the village.

"That must have been terrifying for your father and the other men still in Lifta," I said. "Did they all leave?"

"Yes, there was no choice. When my father came and found us, after Deir Yassin, he was so sad. My mother was crying. She showed him the oranges she brought from our orange tree and the key to our house. My mother and my father were weeping because we lost our house, we lost our village. We had nothing. Nothing. We had left without packing anything because we thought in a day or two we would return.

"After my father found us, he couldn't hold anything in his stomach. He was sick from the stress, from losing everything. They moved him to a hospital and operated on his stomach, but it was not successful. Eventually, he died from grief."

"What happened to you, Yacoub?" I asked.

"Of course, I lost my school. My parents sent me to a school in downtown Ramallah and they gave us breakfast. Maybe my family sent me there to eat because we had nothing. The teacher said to me, 'What's your name?' I said, 'Yacoub Ahmed Mohamed Mousa Odeh.' She said, 'Oh, what a long name you have.' My family was afraid I would get separated from them, so they taught me my long name. Then, if I got lost, people would be able to help me

....

24   Pappé, Ilan. *The Ethnic Cleansing of Palestine*. OneWorld. 2006.

"Seven hundred and fifty thousand of us became refugees in those terrible months."

find them again.

"Soon I had to change to another school. It was in a tent in a soccer field. That winter there was a flood and the tent fell down.

"During all this, we were still living outside, under the fig tree. Then we moved into a room in the Old City. We had only one room and shared the yard with other families. My mother gave birth to my brother Mohamed. When she began having labor pains, the people living nearby put her on a wooden door and carried her to the hospital.

"Soon after, my mother sent me to the UNRWA (United Nations Relief and Works Agency for Palestinian Refugees in the Near East) school in what they now call the Jewish Quarter. Half the day was academic and the other half industrial. It wasn't a serious education. At that time UNRWA had just started. I had to repeat the first two years of schooling because I had moved and lost so much, and then my family moved me again. I had to change schools three more times before I graduated.

"Today is the child of yesterday. And tomorrow is the child of today. So everything I remember—the happy life that we had in Lifta, and then the miserable and fearful events when they kicked us out of Lifta, when they choked the life out of my father, and when I lost two years of my schooling—these things shaped my way in the future. So when I was a teenager, I began to participate in the Arab national movement that said: 'We will struggle to go back home, we will return.' For us young ones this was the only way. And we are still struggling to go back to our homes.

"Today, as we're talking, it's been seventy years since my family was forced to leave our home and our village. But still sometimes I can't sleep because I am going through the details in my mind of what happened to us. I, Yacoub, I am just one example. Seven hundred and fifty thousand of us became refugees in those terrible months."

14
THE "SURVIVAL STAGE": ZEIAD'S STORY

Resistance fighters from many Arab countries joined the all-volunteer Arab Liberation Army, which tried to help defend Palestine. And eventually small forces from the armies of Egypt, Jordan, and Syria came, too. But, according to Pappé, a quarter of the Palestinian refugees had already been forced out of their homes by the time the first outside help arrived.[25] It was too little, too late. Egypt and Jordan were still colonies of England at that point, so their armies weren't allowed to do much to protect Palestine.

At the end of the Nakba, Jordan had control of the eastern half of Jerusalem, including the Old City, and the parts of Palestine we know as the West Bank, including the cities of Bethlehem, Nablus, Hebron, and Ramallah. Egypt controlled the Gaza strip. Israel had everything else. None of Palestine was independent.

In addition to the 750,000 Palestinians who were expelled from their homes between 1947 and 1949, 13,000 Palestinians were killed, 531 Palestinian villages were completely depopulated, and half of all villages in Palestine were physically destroyed. By 1949, only 150,000 of the pre-1947 Palestinian population remained in what Palestinians call "48 Palestine"— the land that Israel controlled at the end of 1948 (as opposed to the land it conquered in 1967). Two-thirds of the refugees who fled Israel went to the West Bank and Gaza. The remaining third

....

25   Pappé, Ilan. *The Ethnic Cleansing of Palestine*. OneWorld. 2006.

scattered throughout Jordan, Syria, Lebanon, and other parts of the world, including the United States.[26]

That started what my friend and colleague Zeiad Abbas Shamrouch calls "the survival phase." Zeiad's parents were forced to leave their home in Zakaria during the Nakba. Zakaria is about ten miles west of Jerusalem, toward the Mediterranean coast. When his family fled, his sister was two-and-a-half years old; his oldest brother was only two weeks old. After many hard months of traveling through mountains, and from city to city, the family ended up in Dheisheh Refugee Camp near Bethlehem. That's where two more siblings and Zeiad were born. At first the families at Dheisheh had no shelter at all; then UNRWA gave them tents. By the time Zeiad remembers life in the camp, the family had a cement room.

"Life in the camp was unbelievably difficult, especially in the winter," he told me. "Our room was eighty-one square feet;

....

26 Visualizing Palestine 101. "Where Palestinians Live Today." September 2019. 10 September 2020 <www.101.visualizingpalestine.org/visuals/where-palestinians-live-today>.

Dheisheh Refugee Camp near Bethlehem in the late 1950s. Many Palestinian refugees, including Zeiad's family, had moved into small concrete rooms built by the United Nations, but some still lived in tents. (Credit: UNRWA Archives).

seven of us lived in that room. The rain seeped in and the cold sneaked through the doors and windows. Many times my family would wake up in the middle of the night because there were several inches of water on the floor. My mother used to say, 'In Zakaria, we loved the rain because we were farmers and we needed it so everything would grow. Now we hate the rain and the cold because we're refugees and far from our land.'

"For many, many years, everyone thought that in a month or two they could return home. This wasn't just true for my parents; most people of the Nakba generation believed our status as refugees was temporary and we would soon get back to our homes. Maybe the Arab army would come and liberate us, or the United Nations would enforce its own agreements."

"What agreements?" I asked.

"The UN has passed many resolutions in support of Palestinian human rights, especially the right of return. One of the earliest, UN Resolution 194, was passed in December 1948, only months after the Nakba.[27] It says that, like others forced into exile by war, Palestinian refugees have the right to return to their homes and their homeland.

"But Israel has never followed UN resolutions, and the rest of the world has let them continue to deny us our rights. When I was growing up, my uncle, my mom, and other relatives didn't want to build houses in the refugee camp or expand the rooms they were living in because they thought they were going back. They wanted to save their little bit of money to rebuild their house in their village."

....

27   For a complete list of UN General Assembly resolutions on Palestine, see: <www.un.org/unispal/data-collection/general-assembly>.

> **"Israel has never followed UN resolutions, and the rest of the world has let them continue to deny us our rights."**

15
AL-NAKSA (THE SETBACK): THE SIX-DAY WAR

"**W**hat about the next war?" I asked Zeiad. "What happened in 1967?"

"From 1948 to 1967, the West Bank, including Jerusalem, was under Jordanian rule," Zeiad explained. "In 1967, Israel attacked Egypt and started a war between Israel on one side and Egypt, Syria, and Jordan on the other.

"At first, Palestinians were excited about the war; we thought the Arabs would win and right away we would be able to go back to our homes. When the Israeli army arrived at our refugee camp, at first everyone thought they were the Arab army. They went to the streets clapping their hands, but then they realized it was the Israeli army.

"The Arab armies were weak. Israel was funded by Britain and the United States, and they had sophisticated military equipment, intelligence, and air power. The war was over in six days. It changed everything for us because the West Bank, which included Jerusalem, came under direct Israeli occupation. Another 300,000 Palestinians became refugees because of the 1967 war. About half of them had already been displaced in 1948, so they were refugees two times over.

"Before 1967, Jordan controlled East Jerusalem, including the Old City, so all the holy places fell under Jordanian rule. When the Israelis came to seize Jerusalem, there wasn't a strong battle to defend it. They say that within the Jordanian army, each soldier

Everyone in Silwan is determined to stay where they are, no matter how difficult things become. They are holding onto Palestine until Palestinians everywhere can come back to their homeland.

only had a few bullets, so they couldn't defend the holy city."

For the Israelis, military control of the Old City was a major priority. They had never agreed that Jerusalem should be an international city. They wanted it to be the capital of Israel. This was their big chance.

On the last day of the war, they destroyed the 800-year-old buildings in the Moroccan quarter of the Old City, after telling more than 650 Palestinian residents they had to leave immediately. Within days, they had created a plaza on top of the rubble so Jews could come worship at the Western Wall. Even today, if you climb up above the Western Wall plaza, you can see the remains of the Moroccan quarter partially hidden underneath. *Mughrabi* is the Arabic word for Moroccan—the Mughrabi Gate was named for the Moroccan quarter of the Old City. So every time Silwanis enter the Old City through the Mughrabi Gate, they are reminded of what happened there.

UN Resolution 242 was passed in November 1967, a few months after the end of the Six-Day War. It stipulated that Israel withdraw from all the territories it occupied in the 1967 war: the West Bank (including East Jerusalem), Gaza, the Golan Heights (part of Syria) and the Sinai Peninsula (part of Egypt). But, in direct violation of the resolution, the occupation continued, and more and more Israeli settlements have been built all over the West Bank, including in East Jerusalem.

People in Silwan, like Palestinians all over the world, remember what happened during the Nakba. When Palestinians left their homes to escape the killing, they lost them forever. That's why everyone in Silwan is determined to stay where they are, no matter how difficult things become. They are holding onto Palestine until Palestinians everywhere can come back to their homeland.

One of Madaa's debka groups practices for a performance. (Credit: Madaa Creative Center)

16

"GIVE THE CHILDREN A LITTLE OF THEIR CHILDHOOD": THE STORY OF MADAA CREATIVE CENTER

The day after the King David tour, Ericka had to leave. I helped her pack and went with her to wait for transportation to the airport. Then I walked back to Madaa. I wanted to connect what we had learned about the history from Yacoub and Zeiad to Silwan. Jawad, director of Madaa and the Wadi Hilweh Information Center, helped me fill in the blanks:

"Here in Silwan," he said, "we lost land in 1948 during the Nakba, but most of our land was lost in 1967. After the 1967 war, we went from being landowners to being hired by Israelis in their factories and their businesses.

"I was born after the occupation, so I don't know anything else, but I see the difference between the occupation in the beginning and now. It's always getting worse. Really, though, there is no nice occupation. All occupations are terrible. It's not only about your house, your land, your work. It's about freedom. And we have never had freedom in this country.

"So from the time I was a child it was very clear to me: I don't want occupation. And from the moment I realized that there was an occupation, I started to struggle against it.

"I was a teenager during the First Intifada.[28] The First Intifada was a huge resistance movement of Palestinians against the

....
28 Intifada means uprising or rebellion in Arabic.

occupation. It started in 1987. Every community was organized. We really believed we would win our independence. My school was in the Old City, and we all threw stones at the Israeli tanks, the armored vehicles, and the Israeli soldiers. That is how I ended up in prison.

"When I got out of prison, I went to Turkey to study. Because of the Intifada, the Israelis had closed Bethlehem University and there was no place else I could go.

"When I came back, the Intifada was over. And Yasser Arafat, who was the head of the Palestine Liberation Organization, had signed the Oslo Accords with the Israelis and the United States [in 1993]. This was very bad for Palestinians."

"People in the US think of the Oslo Accords as the road to peace," I said, "because they called for a two-state solution: one state for Israel and one for Palestine."

"No," Jawad said. "With Oslo we accepted a situation where we let the Israelis control us. The agreement chopped Palestine into more pieces, each with a different set of rules, all enforced by Israel. Israel got full control of external security. Palestinians ended up without control of our borders, our air space, our water, or our other resources—nothing that you need to be independent. On top of that, Oslo postponed the question of who controls Jerusalem and it didn't do anything about Israeli settlers moving into the areas that are supposed to be Palestinian. So the Oslo Accords exacerbated the problem with Israeli settlements in the West Bank that started in 1967. Before Oslo, at least we did not have settlers inside the Palestinian neighborhoods. Today, we have settlers inside many Palestinian neighborhoods, cutting Palestinian neighbors off from each other.

"I left the country again for a few years and then I came back because the Israeli settlers were trying to take my family's house. I was not sure I wanted to stay here. I hated this so-called peace. I felt like we were turning into slaves for Israel. It wasn't only that Israel wanted to control us. It was our decision to be slaves through the agreements we were making. Country after country was running to make agreements with Israel, including Jordan and Egypt. But, I thought, OK. It's enough traveling, I will settle here."

"Why did you start Madaa, the children's center?" I asked.

"We had to do something about what was happening to children and teenagers in Silwan. Their whole lives were about arrests, house demolitions, feeling afraid. The idea was to give the children a little part of their childhood back. Children need a place to be creative, to have fun, to feel safe.

"But if you want to know more about Madaa, come talk to Majd. He's been here from the beginning and now he is our project director."

Jawad took me into Majd's office. Majd Ghaith was a friendly bear of a person, stocky and warm. He invited me to sit down, and went to make coffee. Once we were settled on the couches in his office, I asked him how he got involved with Madaa.

"I grew up right next door. And Jawad was like a father to me. When he started the center, I joined him. I was the first volunteer. As soon as the center opened, I was the coordinator for the courses. There I was, sixteen years old, with so much responsibility. It was a very good thing for me.

"Before the center, you would see a lot of kids playing in the streets. That's how I grew up. But it's too dangerous now, because of the settlers and the Israeli armed forces.

"When we started, we had two courses, an art course and a music course, and thirty-five kids. Now we have thirty-four courses and almost 500 kids. Every day there is something happening here. We lend kids musical instruments and teach them how to play. We have courses in art, foreign languages, and theater. We just finished an animation workshop. We have photography and creative writing courses. We help kids with their schoolwork.

"We provide a place for children to express their feelings. In art class, many of the children will draw a Palestinian flag, what

"We take our youth on trips to the villages that the Israelis destroyed and we show them what happened."

happened when their house was demolished, or a picture of their sister in jail. They can't do that in school. Here they are free to draw whatever they like.

"We take our youth on trips to the villages that the Israelis destroyed and we show them what happened. We tell them: 'These are not separate places—the West Bank, Jerusalem, Gaza, inside the 1948 borders of Israel. Palestine is one nation.' All our activities are about identity.

"Of course, the Israelis—the municipality and the settlers—don't want the center to survive. We had a removal order twenty-four hours after we opened the center. They have come to arrest kids from the center. They have arrested Jawad many times. They want the community to decide that it's not safe to send kids here. A few years ago, when they arrested Jawad and one of the kids at the center, a lot of the kids stopped coming. But we succeeded in bringing them back again.

"When you bring the kids together, it gives them power. And when you bring the kids, you bring the older community. More than 100 women come for classes. We have a women's group that embroiders clothes and makes jewelry. We have computer classes and teach several languages, including Hebrew. The women told us they needed to know Hebrew so they could understand what is happening to their children when they are arrested.

"From time to time, we have a meeting about community projects or hold a celebration. We come at night, sit together, laugh and have fun. A lot of people have gotten to know each other from the center. Now they are good friends.

"If you want an example of the difference we are making in children's lives, look at Dandara, our hip-hop group. Most of the members of the group were here with us from the beginning. The center is their second home.

"One of Dandara's songs is about what Palestinian children are learning about their own history in the schools here. When I was in school, we studied with Jordanian textbooks. In those books, we had a little bit of Palestinian history. They didn't cover it very well—just two pages and you're finished. But it was something.

"Now the Israeli occupation is forcing Israeli textbooks into our schools. In the places where there were Palestinian flags, we see Israeli flags. The history books say that Israel freed the country from the British occupation. Nothing about the Nakba. Dandara talks about this in one of their songs, 'Writing My Own Book.'

"Writing My Own Book"
by Dandara

You took the documents of our houses,
Now you want the ones where our poems are written?
Why are you grabbing our Arab poems?
Why do you want to throw away the national poetry?
What will you leave us with? The romantic poems?
It's not that we are against love
But there are other emotions as well
For example, do you want love?
OK, a couple fell in love
They got married, roses and flowers
They want to live in happiness,
But you took their house, you took their land
So I grab my pen, I write with my pen
No love, no romance, without a homeland

The back cover of Dandara's first CD. Dandara is Madaa's hip-hop group. (Credit: Madaa Creative Center)

17:
"MAKE SOME NOISE": MADAA'S HIP-HOP GROUP

I was excited about Dandara. I asked Majd if I could meet the group. They were practicing that afternoon, so a few hours later he took me to another building down the street that the center used for some of its classes. Nihad came along to translate, although Majd speaks fluent English, too.

The most exciting part of that building had been the media center, but over the winter the roof of the media room collapsed during a snowstorm. Majd showed me the blue tarp that still covered the destroyed roof. Almost all the equipment was destroyed. They were hoping to raise money to fix the roof and replace the equipment.

After Majd introduced me to the group, Nihad and I sat on a bench against the wall to watch them rehearse. We could hear the call to prayer echoing faintly through the building, and Nihad went into a small side room to pray.

The rehearsal was in Arabic, so I couldn't understand what they said, but I could feel the energy and support among the group.

They started with some warm-up exercises that one of the boys led. For the first song they practiced, one of the girls, Hedaya, took the lead. I could see how, with the encouragement from Majd and the other members of the group, her performance got stronger, bigger, and more confident. There was a lot of laughter, but they also listened to each other carefully and worked hard. The youth knew what they had to do, and Majd sat back as they ran the rehearsal. When he did have a comment, their body language and quiet attention reflected how much respect they had for his opinion.

After the rehearsal, two members of the group agreed to talk to me: Hedaya and Odai. On their CD, there's a song where all the members introduce themselves. Here's what Hedaya said:

> My name is Hedaya and I am thirteen years old
> I play the piano and I dance debka
> I hope you will see me become an international artist
> Dancing around the world
> Ala dal'una, Ala dal'una[29]
> I want to show people my culture
> Ala dal'una, Ala dal'una
> I want to show how our olive trees
> Are being stolen from us.

I asked Hedaya how she became a member of Dandara.

"I have been coming to the center since I was eight years old. When I was eleven, some of us got interested in hip-hop. So our teachers at Madaa took us to a youth center in Bethlehem that had a hip-hop group. They showed us how they wrote and performed songs, and how you can use hip-hop to express yourself. Once I saw hip-hop from the outside, I wanted to be on the inside.

"We named our group Dandara, which means 'let's make some noise' or 'let's make it happen' in Arabic. There are seven of us—three girls and four boys. We write the songs together. We have songs about the settlers, about life under occupation. But we also have songs about regular things, about love.

"We pick a topic, then we start by brainstorming. Each of us has our own ideas. Everyone writes a piece of the song, then we bring them all together, and that is how we do it."

"What is your life like outside of Dandara?" I asked.

---

29   Ala dal'una is a traditional Arabic song; the title means "let's go help."

"I go to a school for girls on Salaheddin Street, north of the Old City. To get to school, I have to walk all the way through the Old City, so I see the settlers every day.

"Life in Silwan is hard for everyone, but it is especially difficult to be a girl here. I hate to walk alone in the street when the settlers are around. I feel nervous crossing in front of them. They could do anything to me. Everyone in my family has been beaten or arrested by the police.

"But it's good to be in Dandara. When something happens, when I feel something, I have a way to express myself. I don't have to keep it to myself; now everyone will know.

"We are spreading our message. Last year we went on a tour to France. We got to tell many people what is happening in Silwan. Now they've heard of our village. A lot of people were shocked. They thought they knew what our life was like, but the truth is something else."

"What are your hopes for the future?" I asked. "What are your plans?"

"I want to be a photojournalist. I love taking pictures and getting my message out. I want young people in the United States and other countries to understand what life is like here for us. Then they will tell the US government to stop sending money and weapons to Israel."

Odai was also one of the original members of Dandara. Here's how he introduced himself on the CD:

> Sixteen years old, Odai Qareen
> If I get three wishes like Aladdin,
> Number one, I will free Palestine like Salaheddin[30]
> Number two, I want to be famous so my message will reach you sooner
> Number three, it is really bad up here—three wishes aren't enough, can't I have one extra?

....

30 Salaheddin was a twelfth century military and political leader in the Middle East. He led the Muslim defense against the Crusaders.

> **"What I like about hip-hop is that we can talk about the things that are happening to us."**

"Why are you in Dandara?" I asked Odai.

"What I like about hip-hop is that we can talk about the things that are happening to us. We write most of our songs together, but sometimes I write my own songs, too. I just wrote a song about the settlers hanging around here, about the arrests. The experience that we have is so different from other teenagers. If you go just one or two kilometers to West Jerusalem, the lives of Israeli teenagers are totally different from ours."

"Can you give me an example of how the occupation affects your life?" I asked.

"Two days ago, I was riding on the bus, coming home from school, and the special forces climbed on the bus and made me get off. Then they told the bus driver to go on.

"They took my identity card and made me take off my t-shirt and pants and my boots. Right on the sidewalk in front of everyone.

"They started questioning me: 'What are you doing? Have you been arrested before? Have you been to the police station before?'

"Finally they let me go. I felt like I had been abused. I had so many feelings about that. So I'm thinking of writing a song about it.

"Sometimes I write about other things. I wrote a romantic song. I wrote about a pen. You can use a pen in a good way to write about justice, or in a bad way to create injustice. Maybe I'm a little bit of a poet.

"The media always say that Palestinians are terrorists and that we only use violence to send our message. We want to prove to the whole world that we are human beings and we send our message by music."

The next day was my last day in Palestine. I returned to Sara's house to say goodbye. Nihad couldn't go, so I went on my own. Um Ala'a invited me in. Sara and Lena were there, and the four of us had a lovely, relaxed time, communicating as best we could with Sara's knowledge of English and lots of hand gestures. We hugged and I promised to come back. The settlers stared at me as I left.

I stopped by the Madaa center to thank them for all their help. Then I went back to the guesthouse and prepared to leave. I didn't want to risk being searched at the airport and losing the interview recordings I had made. So I made copies of everything, saving some to the cloud, and sending some home in a box filled with souvenirs.

I took a shuttle from the Damascus Gate to the airport. I saw many people pulled out of line and sent for questioning but, once again, I looked like just another Jewish tourist, and the Israeli security agent at the Tel Aviv airport didn't ask me a single question.

PART II

WE'RE LIVING ON STOLEN LAND, TOO: BACK IN THE UNITED STATES

Corrina Gould. (Credit: Brian Feulner)

18

"MY ANCESTORS CREATED THE FIRST VILLAGE ON SAN FRANCISCO BAY": CORRINA'S STORY

Back home, I realized that being in Palestine made me think differently about the United States. When I saw what Israeli settlers were doing to the Indigenous people and their land in Palestine, I had to rethink those romantic stories about US settlers on the Conestoga wagons heading west—stories from the *Little House on the Prairie* books of my childhood, the *Oregon Trail* computer game of Ericka's childhood, and the US history books I taught each year.

No matter where we live in the United States, Indigenous history has been buried right under our feet. I realized that a fight to re-surface that history was taking place only a few blocks from my house. I live in Berkeley, California, which is Ohlone land. Those are the people who have lived here from thousands of years before the Spanish conquest of California. My house is a ten-minute walk from a parking lot on an upscale shopping street. Developers want to dig up the parking lot and erect a five-story building with shops, apartments, and an underground garage. But the parking lot covers what's left of the West Berkeley Shellmound. According to Ohlone elders and archeologists, the shellmound was built by the earliest inhabitants of the San Francisco Bay area. For the Ohlone people, it's sacred ground.

I went to talk to Corrina Gould, who is Indigenous Chochenyo/Karkin Ohlone, about the West Berkeley Shellmound. Corrina is

"There were grizzly bears and other big mammals, and so many shellfish—oysters, clams, mussels—we could eat as much as we wanted."

the cofounder and lead organizer of Indian People Organizing for Change. She's been working for years to save Indigenous sacred sites in California's Bay Area. We met in her office in the basement of a sprawling Oakland church. The walls were plastered with political posters.

I asked Corrina to explain the history of the West Berkeley Shellmound.

"If you stand in the middle of the asphalt parking lot that used to be the West Berkeley Shellmound, you see railroad tracks, Interstate 80 to San Francisco, apartment buildings, restaurants, the Apple Store. It's all built up. But, according to archeologists, over 5,700 years ago my ancestors created a village here, right by Strawberry Creek, that ran from the Berkeley Hills down to the San Francisco Bay.

"This village was the first place that human beings ever lived along the Bay. My ancestors caught fish and gathered shellfish. We lived next to the sweet, fresh water of Strawberry Creek in tule homes. Tule is a reed that used to grow all over this area. What's now the city of Berkeley was in the center of Huichin territory, which included what are now San Francisco, San Mateo, Santa Clara, Monterey, Alameda, Solano, and Contra Costa counties. The Huichin peoples were one tribe of Ohlone, which occupied coastal regions from the central Bay Area south to Monterey Bay.

"As many as 50,000 people lived here on the central California coast.

"There were grizzly bears and other big mammals, and so many shellfish—oysters, clams, mussels—we could eat as much as we wanted. In the fall, we would walk up into the Berkeley hills to gather acorns along the upper reaches of the creek. We built boats from the tule reeds for fishing, for hunting waterfowl and sea mammals, and for travel and trading around the bay.

"Anything that you see on top of the land now has only oc-curred in the last 200 years. My ancestors lived in reciprocity with the land in such a way that they left a very small footprint. The only thing they left behind were these mounds. They were our burial sites. Because we ate so many shellfish, we had lots of shells. We buried our ancestors in soil and layers of shell and rock. Over thousands of years, these mounds got larger and larger. The West Berkeley Shellmound was about twenty feet high and at least the size of a square block.

"Before the invasion, there were 425 shellmounds in the Bay Area. The West Berkeley Shellmound was the oldest. They were ceremonial and community centers. Sometimes we built fires on top of them to send signals across the Bay—for example, to warn people: 'Don't eat the shellfish now because of the red tide.'

"We lived that way peacefully for thousands of years. Then, at the end of the eighteenth century, the Spanish conquerors and Catholic Church brought the mission system to central California. My ancestors were enslaved in two of those mis-sions, Mission San Jose in Fremont and Mission Dolores in San Francisco. Of course, the Spanish didn't actually build the missions. They enslaved the California natives living close by and made them build their own prison system. It was the first prison industrial complex[31] of California, and my ancestors were the first prisoners there.

"My ancestors didn't give up easily. But imagine people you'd never seen before suddenly coming to your land with strange animals, metal tools, and guns—things that you had never seen before—and creating so much pain. My ancestors never attacked each other in those horrific ways or enslaved each other, so imag-ine what they must have been going through.

....

31   The term "prison industrial complex" was popularized by African American scholar/activist Angela Davis to describe the overlapping interests of government and industry that use surveillance, policing, and imprisonment as solutions to economic, social, and political problems.

"The Spanish brought animals—horses, cows, pigs, sheep, goats, and donkeys— that grazed all our natural foods down to the roots, and many of our medicinal and nutritious plants disappeared altogether. When we got sick, there were no medicines to help us. My ancestors died from the diseases brought from Europe, from malnutrition, and from lack of medicine.

"Many horrible things happened in those days. People were whipped and killed for running away. Whole villages were burned for hiding their relatives. Folks were forced to stop speaking their own language and practicing their religion. Some people believe that 95 percent of the people in our territory passed away.

"Then Mexico took huge swaths of the mission lands from the Catholic Church and gave land grants to military officers like Vallejo, Bernal, and Peralta. My ancestors went from being slaves at the missions to being slaves on those ranches. After the US and Mexico fought over our land, the Treaty of Guadalupe Hidalgo in 1848 said that California Native people were supposed to get some of our land back. But by that time, the United States wasn't interested in creating treaties with Indians or returning our land. Some of the very first laws of California were to exterminate the California Indians. The federal government paid $5 a head and twenty-five cents an ear for California Indians.

"The Gold Rush just made things worse. The forty-niners came here looking for gold. Not everybody could find gold. But you could, on a Sunday with a bunch of buddies, get on horses and go into villages and kill off Native adults and sell the children into servitude back in town. They got from $200 to $300 for a little girl, $75 to $80 for a little boy. Slavery is something that we don't talk about in California, but it happened to California Natives for a very long time.

"I learned some of this history from my mother. Although they were born in Oakland, California, she, my aunt, and my uncle were sent to Chemawa Boarding School in Oregon. The priority wasn't academics, it was assimilation. They forced the children to speak English, taught them basic skills, and sent them to work.

"My auntie, who's eighty years old, told me that she was in boarding school until she was twelve. Then she was placed as a maid in a white home in San Leandro, California. She took care of their kids and did all of their cleaning and laundry. This was in the early 1950s, just before the time of the Montgomery Bus Boycott.

"I was twelve years old when my mother passed away. It was trying to keep the connection with her that pushed me to find out about our history. My mother knew that our ancestors had been at Mission San Jose. So I went there to look for our records and talked to everyone I could find. I discovered that my great-grandfather was one of the last speakers of our language."

"How did you get involved in the struggle to save the West Berkeley Shellmound?" I asked Corrina.

"Over the years, I worked to save several different shellmounds, and one day I got a phone call saying that a developer wanted to build on top of the West Berkeley Shellmound. The shellmound wasn't in good shape. Even before the parking lot, it had been raided by white settlers for shells to pulverize into cement, pillaged

Corrina Gould leading a demonstration at the West Berkeley Shellmound.
(Credit: Brooke Anderson)

"To decolonize is to tell the truth. And to work with Indigenous people is to give the land back."

by pot-hunters to fertilize their yards, and excavated by archeologists. But we know that many of our ancestors are still buried there. We went to the zoning board, the landmarks commission, the developers, doing everything we could to save the West Berkeley Shellmound. We're still fighting."

"What will you do if you win? What is your dream for the shellmound?"

"Our vision is to build a mound that will look like our ancestors' mound on the outside. Inside will be a theater with a 360-degree screen and a film running so you can see, hear, and smell what it was like to be at a shellmound 200 years ago.

"We hope to re-surface Strawberry Creek where it's buried under the cement and plant tules there again to use for basket weaving and boat building. We will create an arbor for dancing and a center so schoolchildren and their families can learn about the true history of this part of California.

"Sometimes the shellmound will be closed to the public so Ohlone people can have a ceremony, and other times it will be open for everybody to come and enjoy. It will be a beautiful green space where people from all over the world can come to talk about Ohlone resiliency.

"A lot of healing has to happen, and we hope that the West Berkeley Shellmound can be part of that. We don't tell the truth about history in this country, that this country is occupied territories of Native people. No matter what inch of land you step on, it's occupied land. It's stolen land."

"Corrina, how do you see the connection between Indigenous struggles here in the US and Palestine?"

"To decolonize is to tell the truth. And to work with Indigenous people is to give the land back.

"It's heartbreaking that you can be on your own land and be homeless and landless—whether that's in Berkeley or Palestine."

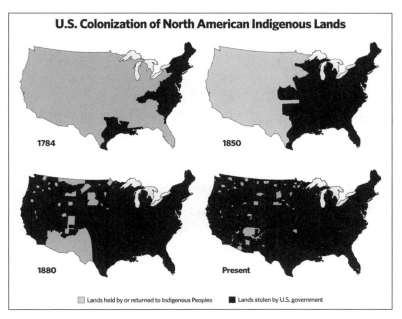

U.S. Colonization of North American Indigenous Lands

1784

1850

1880

Present

Lands held by or returned to Indigenous Peoples   Lands stolen by U.S. government

England, Spain, France, the Netherlands, and Russia all stole Indigenous lands in North America. These maps illustrate land stolen from Indigenous peoples by the US government since the end of the US revolutionary war. (Credit Sam B. Hillard/J. Bruce Jones/Henry Bortman)

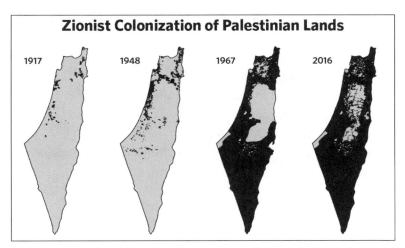

Zionist Colonization of Palestinian Lands

1917   1948   1967   2016

These maps illustrate land stolen from Palestinians by Zionist settlers and the state of Israel. Gray areas indicate Palestinian occupancy, including Palestinians living on land seized in 1948 and 1967. Black areas indicate Israeli colonial settlement, including inside the West Bank (2016 data). (Credit: Visualizing Palestine 101/Henry Bortman)

The colonial conquest of Native American peoples in the United States continues right up to today.

When I first started teaching about Palestine, I would say that the colonization of the United States ended 150 years ago, but that the colonization of Palestine is happening right now, in real time. When Native American teachers heard my presentation, they told me I was wrong. The colonial conquest of Native American peoples in the United States continues right up to today. They told me that colonial conquest only ends when the colonizers recognize what they're doing, stop doing it, take responsibility, and work with the Indigenous people on reparations for the harm. Corrina's work on the West Berkeley Shellmound is one example of a road toward justice.

A similar struggle to acknowledge and pay respect to the true history of the United States took place recently in New York City. This time the ancestors were enslaved and free African Americans who worked and died in colonial New York from the 1630s to 1795.

In 1990, the US General Services Administration (GSA) bought a piece of land in lower Manhattan to build an office building and a parking lot. When they began to excavate the site, they uncovered long-buried skeletons.[32] The GSA's goal was to deal with the human remains as quickly as possible. In their haste to pour a concrete footpath for the office building, a backhoe destroyed several burials.

The African American community was furious. These were their ancestors. Their history had literally been buried beneath the city's streets. The hastily formed Committee of Descendants of the

....

32 This should not have been a surprise. Maps dating back to 1712 note the location of the "Negros Burial Ground," and the location of the burial ground was noted in the environmental impact report required before construction began. See "Bones and Bureaucrats: New York's Great Cemetery Imbroglio," *Archeology Archive*, March/April 1993. 10 September 2020 <www.archive. archaeology.org/online/features/afrburial/>.

Afrikan Ancestral Burial Ground protested by forming a blockade around the site to keep the GSA from pouring the foundation of the building. Black academics joined the protest. After ten years of continuing protests, then-President George Bush ordered the GSA to stop construction. Instead of the office building, a memorial would be built on the site instead.[33]

The 419 bodies that were discovered were sent to Howard University for analysis. Half of them were children less than twelve years old. Black scholars estimate that 15,000 bodies were originally buried at the site. According to anthropologist Michael L. Blakey, who led the research team:

> [These were people] who came from Congo, Ghana, Ashanti, Benin—African states that were war-torn by the slave trade that was driven by the demand for labor in the Americas and Europe... They were malnourished, diseased. Infant mortality was high. Because of their conditions and work stresses and high infant mortality, they were not reproducing. The enslaved population was increasing due to importation [of more enslaved people].[34]

In 2003, some 3,000 participants in a "Rites of Ancestral Return" helped re-inter the ancestral remains (each in a wooden coffin hand-carved in Ghana) at the site, which now includes a museum about the history of slavery in New York City. Nearly 8,000 handwritten messages from the living to their African ancestors were also buried with the remains.

The backhoe destroying African American history in New York reminded me of the reckless excavation at the Givati Parking Lot in Silwan, destroying layer after layer of civilization. And the

....

33   African Burial Ground National Park website 26 April 2019. 10 September 2020 <www.nps.gov/afbg/index.htm>.

34   "Return to the African Burial Ground: An Interview with Physical Anthropologist Michael L. Blakey," *Archeology*, 20 November 2003. 10 September 2020 <archive.archaeology.org/online/interviews/blakey/>.

I wonder if one reason we in the United States, especially white people, don't want to think about Palestine is because it raises questions about our own responsibilities as settlers.

perseverance of the African Americans in claiming and honoring their history reminded me of the resilience of the people of Silwan. But that isn't the only parallel between African Americans in the US and Palestinians in Silwan.

In her book *The New Jim Crow: Mass Incarceration in the Age of Colorblindness*, African American legal scholar Michelle Alexander says that the oppression of Black people in the United States hasn't ended; it has changed form: from slavery, to Jim Crow,[35] to mass incarceration today. She explains that all the things that happen after you're convicted of a felony—not being able to get a job or a place to live because you have to check the "Have you ever been convicted?" box on applications, not being able to get a student loan or food stamps, not being able to vote in many states—has recreated the same kind of caste system, just as segregated, and just as based on color, as Jim Crow.

Israel has a caste system, too. Palestinians have special ID cards that mean they can't travel without Israeli permission, they can't use the same roads as Israelis, they have a different legal system, they go to segregated schools, the list goes on and on.

When US police murder Black people—like George Floyd, Breonna Taylor, Philando Castile, and twelve-year-old Tamir Rice—they rarely face criminal charges, and they're almost never convicted. Just like the Israeli forces when they murder Palestinians.

These startling similarities bring us back to the same issue that Corrina raised: What does it take to end colonial conquest? The US government has never taken responsibility for the impact

....

35   Jim Crow refers to the laws that enforced legal segregation in the South before the Civil Rights Movement.

of white settlers on the Indigenous people who lived on the land that got "settled," or for the impact of slavery, Jim Crow, and mass incarceration on African Americans. There have been no substantive apologies and there have been no reparations—no efforts to heal the damage done over 500 years.

I wonder if one reason we in the United States, especially white people, don't want to think about Palestine is because it raises questions about our own responsibilities as settlers. Whenever our families came as immigrants, and no matter how hard things were back home, they settled on stolen Indigenous land in a country that was largely built by the forced labor of people who were kidnapped from their homelands in Africa and enslaved. Every time an oil pipeline is run on Indigenous land, every time a Black teenager is shot by the police, the trauma is re-inflicted.

Supporters of Palestinian human rights demonstrating to stop Israel's ZIM ship from unloading in Oakland, California, August 2014. (Credit: Leslie Dreyer)

19
WE BLOCKED THE BOAT!

Now that I was back home, it was time to write about Silwan. As I worked on the first draft of this book, there was a crisis in a different part of Palestine—Gaza. Israel launched what they called "Operation Protective Edge," a bombing attack and ground invasion of Gaza that lasted almost two months.

Gaza is a narrow strip of Palestinian land on the Mediterranean, just north of Egypt. It is surrounded and walled in by Israel, which controls all the gates—except one controlled by Egypt—and access by sea. So the 2.2 million people of Gaza are completely cut off from the rest of Palestine and the rest of the world. Gaza used to have an airport, but it was destroyed by Israeli bombs in 2001. Since 2007, Israel has blockaded Gaza, severely restricting access to food, medical supplies, and building materials, and subjected Gazans to periodic invasions and bombing attacks.

During the first weeks of Operation Protective Edge, in July 2014, journalist Mohammed Omer wrote from his home in Gaza:

> At just three months old, my son Omar cries, swaddled in his crib. It's dark. The electricity and water are out. My wife, Lina, frantically tries to comfort him, shield him, and assure him as tears stream down her face. This night Omar's lullaby is Israel's rendition of Wagner's Ride of the Valkyries, with F-16s forming the ground-pounding percussion, Hellfire missiles leading the wind instruments, and drones representing the

string section. All around us crashing bombs from Israeli gun-
ships and ground-based mortars complete the symphony . . .

Shrapnel zings off buildings and cars as another missile
finds its mark, landing on another home. Six more are now
dead. A doctor's house next door was hit by three Israeli F-16
missiles. It's hard to know what the target was. The doctor
was killed, joining his mom and dad, killed in the previous
war in 2008–09. The air strikes are buzzing in my ears and
Lina's. Omar's crying continues. Now the death toll is at 186,
with 1,390 injured. The majority of them are civilians, as
reported by the UN. There is no end in sight.[36]

By the end of Operation Protective Edge that August, 2,200
Palestinians had been killed, including 547 children. More than
100,000 people had lost their homes. According to Defense for
Children International:

There was no safe place for children in Gaza during the Israeli
assault. Children were killed in their homes by Israeli missiles,
while sheltering in schools by high-explosive Israeli artillery
shells, and in the streets by Israeli drone-fired missiles and
artillery shells as they attempted to escape the onslaught with
their families . . . More than 1,000 children suffered injuries
that rendered them permanently disabled . . .

For the children who managed to escape physical injury,
the psychological effects of this latest operation have been
severe and resounding. Many have lost one or both parents,
or other family members. Some have lost their entire extended
families. All have experienced violence, fear, and instability
at close quarters.[37]

. . . .

36   Omer, Mohammed. Shell-Shocked: On the Ground Under Israel's Gaza Assault.
Haymarket. 2015. p. 15.

37   Defense for Children International. Operation Protective Edge: A War Waged
Against Gaza's Children. 16 April 2015. 10 September 2020. <www.dci-palestine.
org/operation_protective_edge_a_war_waged_on_gaza_s_children>.

For those of us who care about Palestine, the news bulletins and videos of what was happening in Gaza were horrifying. Also infuriating were President Obama's support for the attack and the news that Congress gave Israel an additional $225 million in a near-unanimous show of support.[38]

Progressive people all over the world were holding protests, answering the urgent request from Palestinians to pressure Israel to stop the assault. I got an email from Lara Kiswani, executive director of the Arab Resource and Organizing Center in San Francisco (AROC), telling me about a local protest, a plan to block a ZIM ship from docking at the port of Oakland. Would I like to join the coalition planning the action?

I had never heard of ZIM, and I didn't know anything about shipping, but I decided to go to the next planning meeting of the coalition. I needed to do something to support the people of Gaza.

When I got to the meeting, there were about thirty people there: a mix of Palestinian American activists, representatives (many of them Jewish) of organizations with long histories of support for Palestine, younger folks who had been active in the Occupy movement,[39] union organizers, and teenagers from Arab Youth Organizing (AYO), a youth group led by AROC.

Lara explained that ZIM Integrated Shipping Service is Israel's biggest cargo shipping company; it's partly owned by the Israeli government. In addition to shipping food and other items, it ships Israeli-made military and security equipment that end up in prisons and police departments in the United States and around the world. Blocking ZIM from unloading at the Port

....

38 Everett, Burgess."Congress Backs Aid to Israel," *Politico*, 1 August 2014. 19 January 2021 <www.politico.com/story/2014/08/senate-approves-israel-aid-109642>.

39 The Occupy movement focused on income inequality and the lack of democracy in countries around the world. One of its most famous actions was Occupy Wall Street in fall 2011.

of Oakland seemed like a good plan for two main reasons:

1) Block the Boat fit clearly into the international campaign to Boycott, Divest from and Sanction Israel (BDS). The BDS Movement started in 2005, when 170 Palestinian organizations and groups called on the international community to support Palestinian human rights by putting pressure on Israel. They were inspired by the international movement to boycott and divest from South Africa, an important piece of bringing down the apartheid government there in 1994.

2) The Oakland longshore workers, who do the hard work of unloading and loading ships at the port, are members of the ILWU (International Longshore and Warehouse Union), which has a long history of fighting for justice. When ILWU workers refused to unload South African cargo at the San Francisco port in 1984, it helped launch the international anti-apartheid movement. We hoped they would support our demonstration and refuse to unload the ZIM ship.

ZIM docked at the Oakland port every Friday night and unloaded early Saturday morning. We picked Saturday morning, August 16, as our target date to block the boat.

We divided into groups. One group worked with the dockworkers. It was important to build strong relationships with the ILWU because they would be losing pay and risking their jobs if they supported us by refusing to cross the picket line. The youth from AYO played a big role in the group that visited the ILWU hiring hall, waking up early in the morning to get there by 5 AM to talk with the dockworkers about why we wanted to block the ZIM boat.

Another group worked on the logistics of our demonstration. We needed security teams to keep everyone safe, tactical leaders to make decisions, a medical team, chant leaders, a program for the rally at the dock.

The rest of us worked on media and outreach. We had to let as many people as possible know about our protest and explain to them why it was so important. We knew we'd need a good communication system because things could change quickly. Sure enough, late the night before the protest, we all got an emergency text: The ZIM ship, instead of docking in Oakland, spent the night at sea to avoid our picket line. We changed the time of the demonstration to 3 PM, so we would be there for the afternoon shift.

More than 5,000 people showed up with signs and banners for our march to the dock. There was music from the Brass Liberation Orchestra and lots of people with noisemakers. There were families with children in strollers, organizations with matching t-shirts, a shuttle for folks who couldn't walk the mile to the dock. AYO and other Palestinian youth led the march and shouted chants through megaphones: "Block, block, block the boat!" "*Viva, viva, Palestina!*" and "How do you spell justice? BDS, BDS!" Block the Boat happened not long after the murder of Michael Brown in Ferguson, Missouri. One of our chants echoed the support that Palestinians had tweeted to Ferguson: "From Ferguson to Palestine, police brutality is a crime!"

By the time we got to the dock, we heard that the ZIM ship wasn't docking at all that day. Our demonstration was a success. "Our actions today," said Reem Assil, our media spokesperson, "show that genocide and apartheid do not pay in Palestine, do not pay in Oakland, do not pay anywhere!"

Smaller groups went back to the port every day, and the ILWU refused to cross the picket line each time. We kept the ZIM ship from unloading for four days. ZIM abandoned the idea of docking in Oakland and the ship sailed all the way to Russia to unload.

ZIM hasn't been back to Oakland since—we won!

And ZIM hasn't been back to Oakland since—we won!

Soon there were Block the Boat campaigns in Los Angeles, Long Beach, Seattle, Tacoma, Vancouver, New Orleans, and Tampa. People in Gaza watched our demonstration online. They tweeted and Facebooked us, telling us how important it was to see people on the other side of the world supporting them.

It felt wonderful to be part of such a successful protest. And it felt wonderful to be in the middle of so many people who felt connected and committed to Palestine.

20

"ESCALATING VIOLENCE IN JERUSALEM": ZAKARIA'S STORY

Late the following summer, demonstrations broke out all over Palestine, and the suppression by Israeli forces was brutal. In October and November 2015, 2,500 Palestinians were arrested, including 1,200 children.

I worried about the impact on Silwan. How, I wondered, was the situation affecting children's ability to go to school? I called Zakaria Odeh. Zakaria is executive director of the Civic Coalition of East Jerusalem and Yacoub's younger brother.[40] Between daily crises in East Jerusalem and internet problems, it took us a couple of weeks to connect. When we were finally talking, I asked him what was happening. Why were there suddenly so many clashes?

"The escalating violence in Jerusalem—and throughout Palestine—didn't start as a result of some recent killings by Palestinians and Israelis," he told me. "This is the result of all the policies that Israel has been implementing over many years of occupation: land confiscation, house demolitions, settlements, revocation of Palestinian residency in East Jerusalem, constant arrests of our children.

"Our youth have found themselves during the last years in a situation where there's no opportunity, there's no future for them.

....

40   See chapter 13 for Yacoub Odeh's description of living through the Nakba as a child.

Israel has been introducing new laws to suppress and oppress the Palestinians in occupied East Jerusalem and the rest of the West Bank. For example, Israeli Prime Minister Benjamin Netanyahu gave instructions to the police to use live ammunition against demonstrators and against the children who they claim are throwing stones at Israeli soldiers or settlers. After that, we have seen a lot of deliberate killing. In Jerusalem especially it is deliberate execution that has been taking place against Palestinians. In cold blood.

"Although the Israelis claim that in each case there was an attempt to stab an Israeli, witnesses say that sometimes there is a knife, but in most instances there are no knives. Sometimes they have seen the military throw down a knife later.

"Then, they have been closing the neighborhoods within East Jerusalem, separating us from each other. Today in East Jerusalem there are at least thirty checkpoints or barriers. The trip to work that used to take ten or fifteen minutes, now it takes an hour or an hour and a half."

"Are children able to go to school?" I asked.

"Of course schools have been disrupted. Children are not able to reach their schools; if they can reach them, they are one or two hours late. The actions by the police force, the security forces, and the settlers have frightened the children and their families about going to school. In October and November [2015], twenty-two Palestinian children were killed; six in Jerusalem.

"You can't imagine the psychosocial impact on the children of what they see on the street and on TV. They don't want to sleep by themselves. They don't want to go outside because they are worried they might be killed or arrested.

"East Jerusalem is like a military compound these days. First the Israelis brought in 5,000 more troops and then another 1,400 police and special forces. If you walk in the street, you feel the tension: everywhere you see police and military vehicles.

"The teachers are affected by these restrictions, as well, especially teachers who come to school from outside Jerusalem through special permission. The center of Jerusalem, what they call the municipality border of Jerusalem, is surrounded by checkpoints and the separation wall. There are 80,000 Palestinian Jerusalemites who live outside the wall. They hold Israeli-issued Jerusalem ID cards, but now they have to go through a checkpoint every day. There are long delays. Sometimes they can come in, sometimes they are turned away. All of this keeps students and teachers from reaching the schools. So schools are either partially open or not at all.

> **"They often come to arrest the children at four in the morning. They blindfold them, handcuff them, and drive them to a police station or interrogation center."**

"From the beginning, children have been a target for detention and arrest. The Israelis are confronting any peaceful demonstration, even cultural and sports activities. Most of those who are arrested and re-arrested are children under eighteen.

"They often come to arrest the children at four in the morning. They blindfold them, handcuff them, and drive them to a police station or interrogation center. They could hold them for four hours, or it could be for a night or two nights. For many hours, they don't let the children drink or eat, or even go to the toilet. We talk to the families and the lawyers, and they say they make the children do it in their pants.

"They also use house arrests. Sometimes the judge decides a child should stay at home for six weeks, two months, three months. They are not allowed to leave the house at all. They can't go to school; often after they are released they are too far behind and they drop out.

"Many families believe that it's better if the child is held in the prison rather than on house arrest. You know why? Because they make one of the parents sign that they will be with the child all the time, twenty-four hours a day. And they are responsible if

This Palestinian youth from the nearby village of al-Issawiya is under house arrest and is not allowed to leave his home. Credit: (Palestine Information Center)

the child leaves the house. So the parent becomes the police in a way. And this creates some kind of hatred by the child against his parents because it's the parents who can't permit him to leave the house.

"Another punishment they use is internal deportation. If a child lives in Silwan, they punish him by saying he cannot be in his neighborhood with his family for two months: Go to another village, another neighborhood; you are not allowed to be with your family in your house. For most children, if they are in another neighborhood, they lose their right to go to school.

"Then there's the settler violence. They are always around, they are always patrolling. The settlers are another army in occupied territories because all of them are armed. They can do what they want, they are under the protection of the police and the military.

"Many of the parents I talk with say that their children don't want to go to school anymore. These children are seeing their friends being killed, their families, their neighbors. In most of the neighborhoods there are no recreation centers, no places where our children can play sports or do art and music to release tension, to release all that they go through.

"So many of the killings have no reason at all, but even in the situations where the child has a knife, you have to ask: Why would this child go and stab another human being? What has he or she been going through to bring them to that stage?

"This is a natural psychological result of all they're going through, all that they've seen. A child sees his home demolished, or his father is in prison, his brother is in prison. She sees the violence of the settlers, how they attack her family, how they have burned the olive trees and destroyed the harvest of the whole village. These children have to go through a military checkpoint twice every day, wait for who knows how long, then have their bodies and belongings searched. What kind of psychology does this create? What do you expect from this child?"

I was panic-stricken by Zakaria's description of what was happening in East Jerusalem. I worried about everyone I knew in Silwan, especially the young people. Had they been arrested? Were they ok?

I kept thinking about how many Palestinian youth are arrested for throwing stones. That's why Jawad had gone to prison; the first time Zeiad went to prison when he was thirteen, he was accused of throwing stones.

In 2015, the Israeli parliament made throwing stones a felony, with a maximum penalty of twenty years in prison.[41] "A stone-thrower is a terrorist and only a fitting punishment can serve as a deterrent and just punishment," Israel's Justice Minister Ayelet Shaked said.

Knowing that the risk is so great, why do Palestinian children keep throwing stones?

A few years ago, I heard African American scholar/activist Angela Davis speak at an event. She explained that she grew up

....

41   Reuters. "Israel Ramps Up Punishment for Stonethrowers, Palestinians Protest." 21 July 2015. 10 September 2020 <www.reuters.com/article/us-israel-palestinians-stonethrowing/israel-ramps-up-punishments-for-stone-throwers-palestinians-protest-idUSKCN0PV0WW20150721>.

in Birmingham, Alabama, during segregation. As a Black child, she was not allowed in the library, the parks, white bathrooms or restaurants, or in the front of the city's buses.

Her house was on the street that separated the Black section of town from the white section.

"We would sit on our front steps," she told us. "All together, we would run across the street, ring the doorbells of the white houses, then dash back to our side of the street.

"We had to do this. Our choice was to act against segregation, or to internalize the message that we deserved less, that we were less than human. Our psychological survival depended on us ringing those doorbells.

"When Palestinian children throw stones at Israeli trucks and tanks, they are doing the same thing. They are refusing to internalize the message that they are less than human."

21
"OUR EXISTENCE IN SILWAN IS AN ACT OF RESISTANCE": SAHAR'S STORY

Shortly after I spoke with Zakaria, Sahar came to visit Berkeley. She was touring the United States with Madaa's exhibit *Room #4*, which describes, in the words of the children themselves, the conditions they face on arrest. Every Palestinian in Silwan has been taken to Room #4 in the Russian Compound, or has heard terrifying stories about what happens there.[42]

I picked Sahar up at her hotel in downtown Berkeley and brought her to my house for lunch. She was excited that I had Palestinian coffee—"No one in the United States knows how to make coffee," she said—but our coffee grinder wouldn't grind the beans fine enough to make true Palestinian coffee, so she was disappointed once again. Over lunch, she told me how things had changed in Silwan.

"The situation has been much worse, almost unbelievable. We, the staff at Madaa and the information center, we're still human beings. From my own perspective, I can't handle it. I, too, am traumatized. It's not easy for me to hear what is happening to our children. These are my neighbors, these are my nephews, these are my nieces, this is my family. These are all my community members who are suffering.

....

42   Room #4 is where Palestinians are interrogated and often tortured when they are arrested. It is part of the Russian Compound, the central Israeli police station in Jerusalem.

"We are all so worried about our children...but we're staying, and we're doing everything we can to help the children grow up strong and healthy and proud of who they are."

"In the last month, we have been overwhelmed. We are running from one place to another, trying to document what is happening to children and families all over East Jerusalem. Two of the leadership staff at the center were detained overnight and beaten. One of our field workers was arrested for four days. And another colleague, a volunteer, got hit with a rubber bullet on his leg.

"This escalation has been particularly hard on the children. No one is going to school in a regular way. The Israelis have closed all East Jerusalem neighborhoods with roadblocks. To go to school, you need to go through three checkpoints and you're still inside your own neighborhood. My husband takes our children to school, so I feel a little easier, but most families have kept their children home because it's too dangerous to be out on the street.

"Imagine, as a parent, reaching the point that you say to yourself, I know they need to go to school to help their future, but I don't care. I just want them to be safe and alive.

"We've been under occupation since before I was born, and there have been many conflicts in our area. But this is the first time I have felt afraid for myself or my children. Just a few weeks ago, my son's friend was killed while he was waiting on line to take the bus home from school. Killing a child for taking a bus!

"Now, when a parent calls to say that their child has been arrested, first I ask, 'Is he alive?' Only that. Yes, you can break all his bones, but just keep him alive."

"Why do you think the Israelis are arresting so many children? At such young ages?" I asked Sahar.

"They know they are the future. They are targeting our future by targeting our children. They want to make us all leave

Jerusalem. It's not just something they woke up and decided to do. It's a well-planned strategy. They are trying to make our lives unlivable.

"We are all so worried about our children, but we aren't going anywhere. We will stay. Our existence in Silwan is an act of resistance. I don't throw stones. But we're staying, and we're doing everything we can to help the children grow up strong and healthy and proud of who they are. That's the only thing we can do."

PART III

DIGGING DEEPER: RETURN TO SILWAN

22
CHANGES IN SILWAN, CHANGES AT MADAA

Talking with Zakaria and Sahar pushed me to finish the first draft of this book. The next step was to return to Silwan for more voices of Palestinian children and youth. I was finally able to do that in early May 2017. Ericka couldn't come, so I was on my own. Jawad and Zeiad suggested that I stay in Silwan so I would be more part of the community; Jawad promised to find me a place.

By this time, it wouldn't be hard for Israeli security to find my connection to Palestine online: The *Huffington Post* had printed an article I wrote about the destruction of the cultural café, and *Rethinking Schools* published my interview with Zakaria. I carefully deleted contacts from my phone, renamed and hid files on my computer (some of them I still haven't found!) and spent a few sleepless nights worrying about whether I would get through customs.

My plane didn't arrive until almost midnight and the airport echoed with emptiness. When I got to the front of my customs security line, there was a suitcase standing there. I called out to the man ahead of me to see if it was his, then I mentioned it to the customs agent. Maybe this was lucky because it started us off on the right foot. Or maybe the fact that I was an older Jewish white woman was enough. She asked me what I was going to do in Israel. I said go to museums and visit friends. She asked if I was part of a tour. I said no, and that was it.

I spent the night at a hotel near the Damascus Gate and in the morning I took a cab to Wadi Hilweh Street. There was a much

"Life is bitter here and I can't make it sweet. But my tea, I can make it as sweet as I want."

bigger and more solidly constructed construction wall around the Givati Parking Lot—it took up a whole lane of the road. The street was so congested it was hard for traffic to move, and pedestrians were forced into the street.

It was wonderful to see Sahar again. Jawad was away for a few weeks and Sahar was acting director of the center, so she was very busy. As soon as she had a minute to spare, she took me a block down Wadi Hilweh Street to the place where I would be staying. Madaa had lost the space where the women's cooperative used to be to settlers; the women had just moved into a building that also housed some office space, a double apartment with a large cement deck in front. The deck was edged with a high fence twined with grapevines. My temporary home was a couch in the room that would become Majd's office.

Several women came across from the women's cooperative to say hello. They gave me a tour of their space. It was larger than where they used to be; there was a work room with several sewing machines, separate meeting spaces, and a kitchen. They made coffee and tea with fresh thyme leaves. One of the women asked if I wanted sugar in my tea as she put spoonful after spoonful in her own cup. When I said "No, thanks," she explained: "Life is bitter here and I can't make it sweet. But my tea, I can make it as sweet as I want."

I bought pita and yogurt at the little store between the center and my room. Then I walked into the Old City to buy some fruit. I didn't have a map and it was hard to orient myself because the streets inside the Old City looked so different. I was shocked by how much had changed in the three years since my last trip. Areas that housed Palestinian shops only a few years earlier were now filled with upscale Israeli pizza parlors and cafés. One store had costumes so you could dress up as a Jew from Biblical times, become part of a Biblical virtual reality scenario, then get your picture taken as a souvenir.

I walked through the Old City and out the Damascus Gate on the north side. I bought oranges and a ka'ak, a traditional bread ring covered with sesame seeds. Jerusalem is famous for its ka'ak.

Omar, who sold me the bread, spoke English. Business was slow, so we got into a conversation. When I told him I was from the United States, he told me he'd heard about Trump's wall and the attacks on immigrants in my country.

"I'm a teacher in the United States," I told him. "Many of my students are immigrants. Some of them took the risk to travel to the United States without legal papers, to escape violence or because there were no jobs for their families back home. They are always worried about getting caught and being deported. They're afraid to go home to visit—it's too dangerous to come back."

"Where did they come from?" Omar asked.

"All over the world. Yemen, Pakistan, China. But most of my students traveled from Mexico or Central America."

"I have a friend I want you to meet. He's living in fear because he doesn't have the right ID, but he's from this country, only twenty miles away." Before I could say a word, Omar was texting on his phone. A few minutes later, I met Hatem.

23
"I HAD TO TAKE THE RISK": HATEM'S STORY

Hatem was sixteen years old and comes from Hebron. Hebron used to be one of the most vibrant shopping areas in the Middle East. But in order to protect a small number of Israeli settlers, the Israeli military imposed a "principle of separation" on large sections of the city. Most of the Old Quarter was shut down, forcing out hundreds of residents and shop owners, to create a street for the Israeli settlers. Palestinians are not allowed to even walk on the street. Settlers live above the remaining Palestinian section of the market and throw garbage and rocks down onto the stores and shoppers.

I shared the ka'ak with Hatem and Omar as Hatem told me about his life.

"My home is in the Wadi al-Hariya section of Hebron, near the city center. I am the second of six children, and the oldest boy. My father is a shoemaker. Hebron is famous for its shoemakers. My father and two of his brothers have been shoemakers for twenty-five years.

"Even while I was going to school, I worked part-time to help my family. Then my father got sick and couldn't work. I dropped out of school so I could work full-time. After seven months, I decided to come to East Jerusalem because here, I can make more money for my family than I could working in Hebron. In Jerusalem, living is very expensive because everything is Israeli prices, but salaries are much higher than in Hebron."

"We had a ladder and a rope to climb the wall... Suddenly I saw a Jeep full of Israeli soldiers."

"What is it like, living on your own as a teenager?"

"It's hard, I miss my family. And I don't have a residency permit to stay here. If I get caught again, they will put me in prison."

"How did you get caught the first time?"

"It was after I went home to see my family. I was coming back to Jerusalem. There was a group of us; we had a ladder and a rope to climb the wall in Beit Hanina near the Qalandia checkpoint.

"I jumped and hid in a mosque. Afterwards, I left the mosque and started walking. Suddenly I saw a Jeep full of Israeli soldiers. They saw I had a bag of clothes. They followed me, then they got out, grabbed me, and tied my hands behind my back. They threw everything from my bag on the ground. Then they put my jacket over my head and put me in another car.

"They forced my head down. Every time I tried to raise it, they would push it down again. They took me to a place that was like a prison. They hit me and asked me a lot of questions: 'Who is your father? What is your address? How many people in your family? Who else climbed the wall? What taxi did you take from Hebron?'

"The one in charge kept yelling at me because I wouldn't answer his questions. They took my fingerprints and made a file. So if I put my finger on the computer, like at a checkpoint, it will show my photo and everything.

"They kept me for three hours. Then they took me to the Qalandia checkpoint and sent me back to Hebron. After a few days, I paid someone to help me get back to Jerusalem. Now I'm scared to go back home to visit my family."

"How is Jerusalem different from Hebron? Does it feel safer, even though you don't have a residency permit?"

"I think Jerusalem is more dangerous than Hebron. In Hebron, there are settlers and many Israeli police, but not always right where I live. Here, they are everywhere. There is no way to avoid them.

"I have to take the risk because my family needs the money. And I love going to al-Aqsa mosque.[43] I want to go visit my family during Ramadan,[44] but first I will spend a week here to pray at al-Aqsa. Palestinians all over want to pray at al-Aqsa, but the Israelis don't allow them to come, so I will take advantage of the opportunity."

We finished the ka'ak. I thanked Hatem and Omar. Then I took a Palestinian bus back to Wadi Hilweh Street and my new home.

The concrete deck in front of the apartment was too hot and sunny to be comfortable during the day, but that evening it was lovely. As soon as the sun went down, I settled out there with a plastic chair from the kitchen and a book. I looked up the hill towards the walls of the Old City, which shone golden in the twilight. I could tell the Palestinian houses, topped with water cisterns, from the houses of the settlers, hung with blue and white Israeli flags. Although the Jerusalem municipality banned the *adhan* (Muslim call to prayer), I could hear it echoing through the valley. It was beautiful and peaceful, watching the light fade and listening to the wind.

. . . .

43   Al-Aqsa mosque, inside the Old City, is the third holiest site in Islam.

44   Ramadan is the most sacred time of the year in Islamic culture. During Ramadan, Muslims fast, abstain from pleasures, and pray to become closer to God. It is also a time for families to gather and celebrate.

24
"ELAD IS DIGGING UNDER MY HOUSE!"

The next morning, I made myself a cup of tea and a breakfast of yogurt and pita. Then I walked up Wadi Hilweh Street to the center. Sahar wasn't around, but I found Majd in his office. I asked him how things had changed since my last visit.

"There's bad news and good news. Everyday life here in Silwan is only getting harder. Many child arrests. The pace of house demolitions has picked up. And the settlers stole twenty-seven more houses.

"Then there's the impact of the City of David. In the beginning, they were emptying out ancient tunnels that already existed. That caused enough damage. But now they are digging new tunnels. They are digging right under our houses, right here on Wadi Hilweh street.

"At one of the houses, the owner could hear the sound of the earthmovers underneath his house. After a few days, he called the police. When the police came and asked what was happening, he said, 'Elad is excavating under my house.'

"The police brought the municipality engineer to see the house. The engineer didn't tell Elad to stop. Instead, he gave the family an eviction order because their house wasn't safe to live in. It's one more way to evict us.

"We would like to take this to court, but the court will not accept our word for what we can see with our own eyes. Many of us have sneaked down into the tunnels. We can see that what they are doing is huge, lots of machines, lots of building materials. But the court will only listen to an engineer. Hiring an engineer would cost more money than we have, and we would need permission that we know Elad will not give.

"So far, three families have been evicted, but we expect that to happen to many more.

"Then there is the seven-story building that Elad wants to build in the Givati Parking Lot, across the street from the

Madaa youth, mentored by visiting artists, work on a mural. (Credit: Rochelle Watson for Art Forces)

entrance to King David National Park. A few years ago, the Israelis appointed a committee to approve the building. After listening to all the testimony, the committee said no: This project will displace too many people, the developers are not telling the truth about the purpose of the project, and there is no need for it.

"We were so relieved, but then the municipality fired that committee and changed it to different people who gave the decision that they wanted. Now we think they will start building any day.

"The good news is that Madaa Creative Center is growing and growing. We now have three places here in Wadi Hilweh and we have opened centers in two other neighborhoods in Silwan: 'Ein al-Loza and Batin al-Hawa. The idea is to serve as many kids as we can. A lot of kids couldn't get to Wadi Hilweh, so now we're bringing classes and activities to them. We are seeing about 1,000 kids every year, twice as many as a few years ago.

"We try to make sure that we are doing exactly what the neighborhood wants. When we opened the branch in 'Ein al-Loza, the first thing we did was have a meeting for the families there. We asked them: 'What would you like to learn? What would you like to do?'"

I told Majd that one of my priorities was to talk again with the youth I interviewed last time, including Odai and Sara. Majd told me that Odai worked at Madaa now, so it would be easy to arrange to see him. He called Sara's family and set up a time for us to talk the next day. Then Majd introduced me to Bayan Abassi (no relation to Sahar), who also worked at the center. She agreed to come translate for me at Sara's house.

25

"WHEN I HEAR GUNSHOTS, IT'S NORMAL": SARA'S STORY

Abu Ala'a picked Bayan and me up in his car to take us to his house. Three military vehicles and twice as many Israeli soldiers were clustered at the corner, right in front of their house.

I was worried that the family wouldn't remember me, but as soon as we walked in, Lena came barreling down the hall and gave me a big hug. Sara came out of her room and said, "You've come back!"

Sara looked very different now that she was sixteen. She was wearing a long striped dress with a short red vest. The vest had "Minnie Mouse" printed across the front in big letters. The ends of Sara's hair were dyed blonde. At first, she looked pale and didn't want to talk. But soon, with Bayan's encouragement, she opened up:

"I have stepped up to a new phase of life. High school is very different from the school I went to before. In my old school, all the students were girls from Silwan. Now I've met girls from all over Jerusalem and made some good friends. The teachers are older than at my former school; some are understanding and kind, but some are not. The classes are harder. The older you get, the harder things get."

"I've heard so much about the changes in Silwan this year. How have they affected you and your family?" I asked.

"The violence has been more and more, from the settlers and from the police, so that it has started to feel ordinary. When I hear

"My family starts to call: 'Are you OK? Has something happened? Why aren't you here yet?'"

gunshots, I'm not shocked, it's familiar, as if this is a normal way to live.

"Did you see the soldiers right outside our house? They're always there because it's a good spot to overlook all of Silwan. They make me nervous. The settlers have stolen more Palestinian houses nearby. The settlers live side by side with us, but not in the mentality of neighbors. They are enemies.

"The buses used to stop near my house. But the settlers told the municipality that the buses were annoying them, so now this street is one way. It makes it much harder to go back and forth to school."

"Tell me about a regular day," I said.

"I wake up at 6:00 or 6:30 AM depending on what I need to do. If I need to iron my clothes and pack my school bag, I wake up earlier, but if I get ready at night then I can wake up later. I leave home around seven. I don't have breakfast at home because I'm in a rush. My school is very close by, but with bus problems and traffic it takes an hour. Now there's only one bus that comes near my house. If I miss that one, I have to change buses several times and I'm even later.

"My friends call while I'm on the bus and tell me they're waiting for me. They are older than me, in their senior year. They wait at a store near the school. If we have time and money, we buy some breakfast. Then we go to school. But if the traffic is bad or there are extra checkpoints or problems with the police, I don't get there until the middle of first period at 8:30 or 9:00. Sometimes a lot of girls arrive late, so the teacher knows it's not our fault, but sometimes she gets angry.

"Getting home takes even longer. My family starts to call: 'Are you OK? Has something happened? Why aren't you here yet?' By the time I get home, I'm exhausted, which makes studying hard.

"My mother always reminds me to wear many layers of clothing when I go out. Sometimes the Israelis undress girls after they shoot them. Afterwards, they take pictures of them naked and put the photos up on social media. They shot some girls from my school. I have always dressed conservatively when I go out, but now I wear layers and layers of clothes because I'm so afraid that might happen to me.

"My family has high hopes for me after high school. They want me to go to college. My older sisters got married early and didn't go to university, so I'll be the first one. The problem is that I don't know what I want to do. I have a different idea every day. Sometimes I think I want to be a journalist. But it's hard to get a job in journalism and it's a very dangerous job—the Israelis often shoot journalists. Sometimes I want to be a nurse, but I'm taking mostly literature classes in high school, not science classes. So I don't know. I might try to go to university outside of Palestine, to see something new and feel what it's like not to live under occupation."

While we were talking, Abu Ala'a came in with refreshments. First he brought us colored cold drinks in small glasses: pink, green, and yellow. A little later, he brought us a tray with cut-up watermelon and dates. We stayed for a while, chatting with the family and playing with Ali's little boy. He was so much bigger than the last time I visited. Now he was walking and talking. But he still loved to sit in his Aunt Sara's lap.

As Abu Ala'a showed us out, he took us downstairs to show us the changes he had made to the house. He had created a beautiful kitchen and living area, with big windows—the largest I saw in Palestine—and balconies on two sides. You could see virtually all of Silwan spread out below.

He gave Bayan directions for how to walk back to the center. On our way, we talked about how different the Israeli houses look from the Palestinian houses—everything new and fancy, with lots of plants growing because the Israelis get as much water as they want. The Palestinian houses are crowded, all piled on top of each other because it's impossible for them to get more space

"I'm not allowed to be here!"

in Silwan, and hardly anything growing because water is so scarce and expensive.

"This all looks like new development, too," I said. "I don't remember this from the last time I was here." Suddenly we realized we had taken a wrong turn. Everything looked different because we had stumbled into a new section of the City of David. There were groups of Israeli children coming down the stairs toward us, chattering in Hebrew. We could see a guard station up ahead.

"I'm not allowed to be here!" Bayan whispered to me frantically. We tried climbing a different set of stairs, but it just took us to the plaza area of the City of David. Bayan asked me to talk to the guard, ask him how to get out. He told me to go through the plaza. We had no choice.

So I took Bayan's arm and we walked through the plaza, past the ticket counter and the birthday room and the gift shop. I could feel Bayan shaking next to me.

"Excuse me," I said over and over, to the school children and tourists who clogged the space. We pushed our way through. No one stopped us. Finally, we passed under the entranceway with David's golden harp and were back on Wadi Hilweh Street.

"Now I have to worry about what the Palestinians are thinking about me, coming out of that place," Bayan whispered. "That was terrifying."

"I was pretty nervous myself," I answered. Now we were both shaking. We walked quickly down the street to the center, which felt more like a refuge than ever, and collapsed on the chairs in Bayan's small office.

Many of the older girls and women in Silwan wear a hijab, but not all of them. Bayan is one who doesn't. I couldn't help thinking how different our experience might have been if she had been wearing a hijab and was immediately identifiable as Palestinian.

The next night, Sahar made *maqluba* and brought it to the deck for dinner.

Maqluba is a traditional Palestinian dish cooked in a large pot with careful layers of meat, potatoes, eggplant or other vegetables, and rice. When it is done, it is turned upside down onto a serving platter and has a beautiful crust on the top. (*Maqluba* means "upside down" in Arabic).

In addition to Majd, Sahar, Bayan, and me, there was a couple from France who had been to Silwan many times in the past—Nadine was doing massage on some of the Silwani women, to help them deal with the ongoing grief and stress of their lives.

"This is delicious," Nadine said. "What spices do you use to make it?"

"It depends where in Palestine you're from," Sahar said. "Maqluba always has allspice and cardamom. I add cumin and cinnamon and a little turmeric. In Hebron they use lots of turmeric, so the rice is very yellow."

As we added chopped salad and yogurt to our plates, Bayan said: "Yogurt is something else that is different depending on where you are in Palestine. My mother can tell where yogurt is from just by tasting it."

"The best is Bedouin yogurt," Majd said. "It's made from sheep's milk."

A bell rang outside, and Majd ran down to buy everyone Palestinian ice cream, four different colors in a cone. As we licked our ice cream, he told us that the house behind us belonged to a man who saved for twenty years to be able to extend his house upward. He had just finished the addition when the Israelis told him to tear it down because he didn't have a permit. If he didn't tear it down himself, they would tear it down and charge him for it. So he tore it down himself and left Silwan to rent an apartment in a refugee camp.

By now it was dark and cool on the deck. As we thanked Sahar for the wonderful meal and said goodnight, Bayan and I made plans to go to her house the next day after work to meet her family and some of her cousins.

Bayan Abassi. (Credit: Madaa Creative Center)

26
"I'M IN LOVE WITH MY CITY": BAYAN'S STORY

Late the next afternoon, Bayan and I began the walk to her house in the 'Ein al-Loza neighborhood of Silwan. We walked down the sharp hill of Wadi Hilweh Street, past the steel gates and barbed wire that now surround the Silwan Spring so that no Palestinians can enter, and then up and over the next hill. We walked along a cliff above a trash heap, through alleys and up and down narrow streets. As we walked, Bayan told me about her family:

"I'm twenty-five years old. I have five sisters and I am the youngest one. Then I have two brothers who are younger than I am. They are both in high school."

"Has the situation in Silwan changed since you were a child?"

"Absolutely. When I was very young, the settlers weren't that strong. They were nervous to be in Silwan and they weren't that aggressive.

"The first time I realized that everything was different was six or seven years ago. There was a boy named Islam. He was nine or ten years old. His sister was a friend of mine. He was crossing the street and a settler hit him with a car. He hit him twice. I saw the video—it's clear he did it on purpose. It's very hard to watch.

"Since then, every part of our lives has gotten harder. After I finished high school, I studied at Al Quds (Jerusalem) University. Look, you can see it there on the other side of the wall. It's very close to my house."

"Because of the wall, it took me an hour and a half each way, and I had to get through a checkpoint."

I looked in the direction Bayan was pointing. Sure enough, I could see Israel's apartheid wall and beyond it, the white stone buildings of the university.

"Before the Israelis built the wall, it would have taken me fifteen minutes to get to the university from my house. Because of the wall, it took me an hour and a half each way, and I had to get through a checkpoint."

Bayan stopped walking and hesitated for a minute. Then she said: "This is the first time I've talked about this event. It was my first year at the university; I was eighteen years old. I was a very, very shy kid. Maybe because I'm the youngest daughter, they treated me like a baby. I did not know about relationships or sex. I had never been in a situation where there was sexual abuse.

"That day I accidentally left my ID card in the house. For Palestinians who live in Jerusalem, we can't go without our identity card. You could go to jail if you don't have it. I had a university card that had my ID number on it. I told the soldier at the checkpoint that I forgot my ID card in the house, and I gave him the university card.

"He started laughing and making obscene gestures with his hands at me. I was shocked. No one had ever treated me like that. I couldn't deal with it. Especially since he was a soldier. When you work for an organization, you are a representative of that organization. And he had all the power. There was nothing I could do.

"Finally, he let me past the checkpoint, but he made me feel horrible about myself. My friend was at the checkpoint with me. She told me, 'He's just being a jerk. Don't worry.' She tried to calm me down. But I couldn't stop crying. And I never told my family.

"That was the first time that happened to me. But things like that always happen at the checkpoint. For example, my girlfriends who wear hijab, they make them take off their scarves and some-times more of their clothes."

"How terrible," I said. "And to know you have to go back the next day, and the day after that. But you kept going, right? What was your major?"

"I got my undergraduate degree in psychology. Now I'm studying for a master's degree at Birzeit University. Although it's less than twenty miles, I have to change buses so many times: One bus from Silwan to the main bus station near the Damascus Gate [just north of the Old City]. From the Damascus Gate to Ramallah, I take another bus. Then from Ramallah to Birzeit, I take a shuttle. On the way back, I take the shuttle from Birzeit to Ramallah, one bus from Ramallah to the checkpoint, one from the checkpoint to the Damascus Gate, one from the Damascus Gate to Silwan. I get migraine headaches, so a headache when I have to take all those buses is horrible. If nothing goes wrong, it takes two or two and a half hours to get there, about three or three and a half hours to get home.

"The checkpoint at Ramallah is the worst. Especially in the wintertime when it's rainy and cold. They always have the air conditioning going. Because it's cold out and you're wet from the rain, it's freezing. Sometimes they close the checkpoint and I have to stay at my friend's home in Ramallah because I can't get home.

"I have a lot of friends in Ramallah. I would love to go hang out in a café and spend time with them after school. But I can't because it takes me so long to get home.

"One day last week I had to study at the library after class. It had been a long day: I was at my job at Madaa in the morning, then I spent hours getting to school, then class, then the library. I left the library about seven at night. Because I was so tired, I fell asleep on the bus.

"When we reach the checkpoint, all Palestinians younger than fifty-six have to leave the bus and walk to the checkpoint. But I was asleep.

"The United States, Europe, the whole Western world supports Israel. So far, all their talk about democracy and human rights hasn't given us anything."

"Suddenly a woman soldier pushed me really hard. I woke up, shocked. I told her I was asleep, so I missed the station where we should get off the bus. She took my ID and she pushed me off the bus.

"She was yelling at me in Hebrew. I don't know very much Hebrew, but I know she said, 'You shouldn't sleep. It's your fault, not mine, if you go to sleep.'

"There were two tourists from France. They had French passports, but their origins were Arab. It was the first time in my life I saw the soldiers force tourists to get off the bus.

"The soldiers yelled at them in Hebrew, too, but they only spoke French and a little bit of English. So I showed them the way to the checkpoint. Eventually I got through, but it was a very long wait."

"That sounds so stressful," I said. "I can't believe you're so committed to going to school you're willing to go through that every day. Are you still studying psychology?"

"The focus of my master's degree is democracy and human rights. I chose it because I thought we could make accomplishments for Palestine through international law. But now that I have a deeper understanding of the history of the fight for human rights, I think the situation is hopeless. The United States, Europe, the whole Western world supports Israel. So far, all their talk about democracy and human rights hasn't given us anything. I hope, I really hope I'm wrong, but that's what I see."

"Do you think about moving someplace else where life is easier?"

"Despite everything, I'm in love with my city. I can't live outside Jerusalem. Last summer I got an internship in Jordan. I went to Amman for one month, and then I began choking. I wanted to come back! I didn't even finish my internship. I decided to study at Birzeit instead.

"We just have to stop the settlers and the settlements from taking over Palestinian homes and neighborhoods. Their dream is to make us leave—to make all of us refugees from Palestine. But it's our land. We can't let them take it. Every time they take a home in Silwan, everyone is very sad and shocked. It's our land.

"They already have so much of our beautiful land. They have Haifa, they have Jaffa, they have the coast—why are they coming here to take our homes and throw the families out on the street? They have so much. Why are they always trying to take more?"

All this time, we were walking. Finally, up one more hill and around one more corner, we were at Bayan's house. Her mother came out to greet us and welcomed me in.

The living room walls were white with recessed blocks of pale blue; the ceiling was decorated in a complicated geometric pattern in plasterwork.

"The ceiling is beautiful," I said.

"My father is a craftsman. This is the work he does," Bayan told me.

Her mother brought cold drinks. She and Bayan's two older sisters sat talking with us for a while. Then we had dinner: a large tray of yellow rice with ground lamb, potatoes, vegetables and chicken, garnished with almonds and served with yogurt. It was delicious.

27

"MY FATHER IS PART OF THE HUNGER STRIKE": NOURA'S STORY

Bayan knew that I was interested in the impact on families of the many Palestinians in prison, often for long or life sentences. So she invited Noura over to talk with me. Noura's father has been in prison since she was only a few months old, serving twenty-six life sentences plus ten years. This means that the family can't get his body back, even after his death. After Noura's father went to prison, her mother got divorced and married someone else. As a result, she lost custody of Noura, who lives half-time with her maternal grandmother, and half-time with her paternal grandmother.

Noura came over after dinner. She looked nervous, twisting her hands together in her lap. She told us at first she wasn't going to come, but then she decided she wanted people in the United States to know her story.

"Tell us something about your life," Bayan urged.

"OK. I'm fifteen years old. I go to al-Shamila School in Ras al-Amud, a Palestinian neighborhood southeast of the Old City. It's just for girls. Next fall I start at a school in the Old City; it's very old with a long history.

"Silwan is beautiful. Please invite students in the United States to come visit and learn about our history. I can see from pictures that the United States is beautiful, too, but it is different here.

"Now the settlers are trying to ruin Silwan. Because of them, I

"It's hard to visit the prison ... I can see my father, but it's only for an hour. The visit is behind glass. We can't touch each other or be close."

have missed my father since I was four months old. That's when he was arrested. One of my uncles was arrested, too. This has made my life very difficult."

"Are you able to visit him?" I asked.

"Yes, but it's hard to visit the prison. We have to leave at five in the morning to get there in time, and we don't get back until six at night. We get inspected what feels like a thousand times. First we show our ID, then they send us to a room to take off our shoes. Women soldiers do a body search. Then they send us to another room to go through screening machines. Finally, I can see my father, but it's only for an hour. The visit is behind glass. We can't touch each other or be close.

"It's the whole day for those few minutes. After every visit I have a headache, my back hurts and I'm exhausted. I used to be able to visit every other week, but the Israelis changed the rules about a year ago, to punish us for the clashes in Jerusalem, so now I can only visit every six weeks.

"Did you know that there is a hunger strike in the Israeli prisons? It's happening right now. Hundreds of the Palestinian prisoners, including my father, aren't eating or drinking. One of the demands of the prisoners' hunger strike is more frequent visits, so I hope I will be able to visit more soon.

"My grandmothers, my uncles, my whole family takes good care of me, but I hope the situation will get better and my father will be free."

I asked Noura about the rest of her life.

"I like debka and I do it all the time," she said. "I just won an award in a regional debka contest. But my priority now is school. I love school. My team won first prize in a science competition. Students from twenty-two schools competed, and we won. Our project was on the effect of hormones on plants. We read on the internet that several scientists claimed that female hormones will make plants grow faster. That sounded like a dangerous idea to us, so we decided to test it out. We developed an experiment to dissolve the hormones in liquid and use it to water carnation and lentil plants. Our experiment proved that the hormones didn't help the plants grow; in fact, it killed them. I love doing experiments. I hope to become a medical researcher."

After we finished talking with Noura and she went home to finish her homework, Bayan took me up to the roof of her house. It was lovely up there; you could see far in all directions. There was a small swimming pool with a ceramic tile bottom. I could imagine how nice it would be to cool off there, especially at night when you could see the stars and the lights from the city.

Bayan pointed out where Noura's family's house used to be. When Noura's father was sentenced, the Israelis demolished the house as part of the punishment. When the family tried to clear away the wreckage, the Israelis wouldn't let them do that. They wanted to keep the signs of the destruction so the family and the neighborhood would be continually reminded.

One of Bayan's cousins joined us on the roof with his wife and toddler. He called me a cab. While we waited for it to come, we hung out, playing with the baby and talking, enjoying the cool night breezes. Soon the cab came. The cab driver wound up and down the hilly streets on roads so narrow that he had to pull onto the sidewalk when a car came in the other direction. I had no idea where we were, and I started to get worried because he didn't speak any English and I didn't speak any Arabic. But soon we were in front of the apartment. As I let myself in, my cell phone started ringing.

"Hi, sweetie, how ya doin'?" rumbled a deep voice. It was my friend Kalima.

Kalima was in prison in California for forty-six years. When he was arrested and convicted in his early thirties, he was doing armed robberies—he was a very angry and violent man. But he was at San Quentin prison when George Jackson, Geronimo Pratt, and other leaders of the Black Panthers were there. They talked about Black history and gave him books to read. He was so excited to understand his life and the world in a new way. The more he learned about Black history, the more political he became, and the more he understood why he had been so angry. He eventually converted to Islam and changed his name to Kalima. By the time I met him, he was a gentle, thoughtful man whom many of the young men in the prison saw as a nurturing father figure.

For many years, Karen and I were part of a small group of supporters who were trying to help him get out of prison. We visited once a month, and tried to respond to the many letters he sent. The visiting room was run by cold and hostile guards. It was filled with Black and Brown prisoners and their families. I was never sure which was harder to see—the young men trying to connect with their children, surreptitiously holding hands with their wives and girlfriends under the table, or the old men like Kalima, pushing walkers, bent over from years of prison life.

Kalima's requests for parole were turned down twenty-six times. Then, twice, he was granted parole and thought he was going to get out. Each time, only a few days before his release date, the governor denied his parole. He was devastated each time.

Just before I left for Palestine, Kalima, who was then seventy-nine years old, got a new parole date. He was due to be released while I was gone, but we were all worried that the governor would pull his date again.

For years, he had been planning his first meal in freedom. And there he was on the phone, talking to me while he was eating his freedom meal: fried trout and a chocolate milkshake. It felt like a miracle. I started getting photos on my phone: Kalima with Karen, Kalima with the chocolate milkshake, Kalima with all the friends who had gathered to celebrate his release.

I burst into tears. They were tears of happiness, and also tears of grief for Kalima, for Noura and her father, for all the prisoners in Palestine and in the United States. I had learned so much about the US criminal justice system from Kalima. Seeing how arrests and incarceration were affecting families in Silwan, I felt overwhelmed by the parallels.

28
"WE DIDN'T WANT TO SHOW THEM WE WERE AFRAID": NIDAL'S STORY

Early in my trip, I reminded Sahar that I was hoping to interview a teenager who had been on house arrest or spent time in prison. In addition to the many things she already had on her plate, I think she was reluctant to expose a child who had been through such a traumatic experience to the added trauma of talking with me.

The day after I went to Bayan's house, I was sharing lunch with the women in the crafts collective. A few days before, I had seen the sewing teacher balanced precariously on a chair at the end of our deck. She was picking leaves from the grapevine growing up the wire fence that kept us from falling off the deck onto the street below. Now she had brought stuffed grape leaves into the crafts collective, and I was invited. Those were the best grape leaves I've ever tasted. Stuffed with rice, greens, and spices, they were much smaller than the grape leaves I'm used to eating in the United States, and cooked with slices of fresh tomatoes. It was the spiciness and juiciness that made them so delicious. She served them with yogurt and baba ghanoush.[45]

As I was eating, Sahar rushed in to find me. "Hurry," she said. "I have a child who is here to talk with you about his time in prison."

....

45   Baba ghanoush is an eggplant dish popular in Palestine and throughout the Middle East.

"They kept yelling: 'Confess! Confess! Confess!'"

Nidal was sitting in the walk-through kitchen of the office where I was staying. You could see in the way he held his body that he had lived through something horrible; something he had not been able to recover from. His head was crisscrossed with scars.

I thanked him for being willing to talk with me and set up my tape recorder. He spoke so softly that I asked him several times to talk a little louder; I was afraid we would lose his story. Sahar translated for us.

"Please," I began, "tell me something about your life before you were arrested."

"I was in sixth grade. I had a happy life going to school and being with my family and my friends.

"Then one night when I was twelve years old, they came at 4:30 AM and took me from my home. They took me to Room #4 at the Russian Compound. The first day they asked me lots of questions. Then I was beaten and tortured. They kept yelling: 'Confess! Confess! Confess!' But I had nothing to confess, so I kept getting beaten. I was all alone without my parents or a lawyer.

"They tortured and interrogated me for four days, then they sent me home on house arrest. I was on house arrest for ten months. I wasn't allowed to go outside the house. No school, no friends, nothing. My friends were going out and having fun, playing soccer in the neighborhood, and I couldn't go with them. It's torture knowing freedom is out there and yet you can't reach it.

"How did that affect your relationship with your parents?"

"I was fighting with my parents all the time because I wanted to go out and they wouldn't let me. They didn't have any choice. Every day, the cops would show up to check whether I was in the house. We were under pressure all the time. It was a hopeless feeling, like I was choking.

"Every month or two, I had to go to the Israeli military court for my trial. After going to court seven times, they sentenced me to a year and a half. I was the youngest one who got that sentence. The ten months I already spent on house arrest didn't count. I had to start my sentence all over again in the prison.

"After I was sentenced, but before they sent me to the prison, they sent me to the interrogation center at al-Masqubia [police station in West Jerusalem]. For thirteen days they left me suspended."

Sahar and I stared at each other as she translated Nidal's words. "What do you mean?" I asked him.

"For thirteen days they left us all day handcuffed, lifted up, suspended against the wall. We had no food or water. And they would torture us by placing a glass of water in front of us and humiliating us for being unable to reach it."

I knew that my job as a journalist was to sit quietly, to ask questions and let Nidal tell his story. But it was so hard not to cry, not to scream at what had happened to Nidal as a thirteen-year-old child. How could anyone do this?

"Why did they do this to you?" asked Sahar. "What did they want?"

"To torture and humiliate us. After the thirteen days, they sent us for three days to a jail in Ramla, and then to Hasharom prison. After a month, my family was finally able to visit me."

"What was it like in the prison? Did you have school?"

"I was in a section of the prison that was high security. We were all younger than eighteen. The food was terrible. It was winter, but they had the air conditioning going. We had no warm clothes, and not enough blankets. They didn't allow our parents to bring us jackets or more blankets.

"Because we were Security Level Five, we weren't allowed to have any education. I had nothing to do all day but waste time and talk with some friends. My friend Ayad was with me the whole time. We became like brothers. We didn't want to show them that we were scared, so we tried to keep ourselves strong.

"After the year and a half had passed, it was the day we were supposed to be released. We waited all day and nothing happened. At 4:30 in the afternoon, Ayad and I lost hope that we would be released. We changed back into the clothes we wore every day in prison.

"Finally they came and gave us papers to sign and we were released. My family was waiting at the prison gate. My family and many people from Silwan. There was a march back to my house. Even during this celebration, the Israeli police were all around us. They took away the Palestinian flag that someone was waving."

We just sat for a moment, the three of us. It was hard to go on. Finally, I asked: "What was it like, adjusting back to life in Silwan?"

"I went to the [Israeli] Ministry of Education and tried to get back into school. They wanted me to go back to the sixth grade. But I was sixteen years old and I had been through so much; I couldn't be in a class with twelve-year-olds. Sahar and other people at Madaa tried to talk to the authorities, but they wouldn't let me back into school.

"Now I'm almost eighteen. It has been difficult. Everything has changed around me. I'm still trying to collect myself. I work in a bakery. And I've been arrested twice since I got out of prison."

"This is something they do," Sahar explained to me. "We know from statistics that they target people, including children, who have been arrested before. It's like a stigma. Whenever something happens in this neighborhood, the first people who are arrested and interrogated are the people who have a record."

"The first time they wanted to arrest me after my release from prison, they came to my work," Nidal said. "When I didn't agree to go to the interrogation center voluntarily, they arrested my mother and took her in. So I went immediately. They interrogated me and then let me go.

"The second time, there were clashes. They took me from my home in the middle of the night and kept me for two days. I feel like it will happen to me again any minute.

"On November 29, 2015, during the clash- **How could** es here in Silwan, they shot and killed Ayad. He had two bullets in his chest. I have had two **anyone do that** best friends in my life, Ayad and Mohamed. **to children?** When Ayad was killed, it left me with a lot of emptiness. At the same time Ayad was killed, Mohamed was arrested.

"Just last week, Mohamed was released. Since then, I have been with him day and night at his house."

"What do you want me to tell teenagers back in the United States, Nidal?" I asked.

"Tell them that our life is difficult. No one escapes being arrested. All the confrontations and house demolitions. The checkpoints even on the way to school and back. Now they are targeting women, which provokes us even more because of the disrespect. It's not easy what we are facing here."

I thanked Nidal for sharing his story; he was in a hurry to get away. I heard many painful stories in Palestine, but Nidal's upset me so deeply, I didn't know how to deal with what had happened to him, to come to any peace within myself afterwards. That evening, I sat in my plastic chair on the deck, watching the lights flicker on the hill up to the Old City. Who are these people? I wondered. How could anyone do that to children?

As the night darkened, I heard the adhan echoing in the distance. And then the air was filled with Israeli music and singing, coming from several directions, different songs clashing and competing with each other. It was so loud I knew they were blaring from loudspeakers, not drifting from air-conditioned rooms. One more form of colonial conquest, this time taking up all the space in the air over Silwan.

29
WHAT DOES RESPONSIBLE ARCHEOLOGY LOOK LIKE?
A VISIT TO EMEK SHAVEH

A lot of my understanding of how archeology has functioned as a tool of colonial conquest in Silwan (and throughout Palestine) comes from the reports of Emek Shaveh, an organization of Israeli archeologists. They see their goal as:

> *defending cultural heritage rights and protecting ancient sites as public assets that belong to members of all communities, faiths, and peoples. We object to the fact that the ruins of the past have become a political tool in the Israeli-Palestinian conflict and work to challenge those who use archaeological sites to dispossess disenfranchised communities.*[46]

I wanted to talk with Emek Shaveh about what they thought was going to happen to Silwan in the future, so I made an appointment at their office in West Jerusalem.

Looking at the map, it didn't seem far, so I decided to walk. I wound my way through the Old City and out the Jaffa Gate. As I walked toward West Jerusalem, I could see how rapidly the landscape was shifting. Beautiful old cemeteries and archeological sites and then, everywhere, earthmovers and construction. The hill I was climbing passed through a fancy modern complex

....

46 Emek Shaveh. "About Us." 10 September 20 <www.alt-arch.org/en/about-us/>.

of offices, a theater, and even a windmill, presented to Israel by Dutch Christians.

Suddenly there were trees, grass and flowers, broad streets, large houses. This is the part of the city that Israel seized and has held since the Nakba, when almost all Palestinians were expelled.[47] Before 1948, it was one of the wealthiest Palestinian areas.

On many of the houses, you could still see indications—in the architecture, the stone and tile work, the engraved lettering—that these had been Palestinian homes. I walked through a blocks-long park with a large children's playground and paths weaving through the green landscape of trees, bushes, and grass. Jerusalem is so beautiful, and the Palestinian history is barely beneath the veneer. I could only imagine how painful it must have been for the Palestinian residents to be forced out of their homes and neighborhoods.

Just a few blocks from Emek Shaveh's office, I came upon a street named Sokolov. My last name is Sokolower—so similar. Was the street named for an ancestor of mine? I ended up as a white settler in the United States, but I could have ended up as a white settler in Palestine. If that had happened, what would I be doing about Israel's conquest of Palestinian land? Would I be living in a house stolen from Palestinians? Of course, those questions led me to another: What am I doing about being a white settler on land stolen from the Ohlone? I made myself a promise to think more about that question when I got home.

....

47   By the end of the Nakba in 1948, Israel controlled West Jerusalem and Jordan controlled East Jerusalem. In the 1967 war, Israel conquered East Jerusalem. The United Nations has consistently refused to recognize Israeli control of any of Jerusalem. According to the UN, a "comprehensive, just, and lasting solution" needs to be determined by negotiation. See "United Nations Position on Jerusalem Unchanged, Special Coordinator Stresses, as Security Council Debates United States Recognition of City," UN Security Council Meetings Coverage, 8 December 2017. 10 September 2020 <www.un.org/press/en/2017/sc13111.doc.htm>.

Emek Shaveh's offices were a few rooms in a modest building divided among several nonprofits, a striking contrast to the large modern office buildings only a block away. Talya Ezrahi, external relations coordinator at Emek Shaveh, filled me in on their perspective on Elad and the City of David National Park:

"They're always expanding, always building, always digging," Talya began. "Now they've built an amphitheater near the plaza at the City of David. The plan is to turn it into a music venue with rock stars and local performers. It's another way to take over the space, this time with cultural events.

"They've opened up a new tour, called the Pilgrim's Trail, that goes from the Silwan Spring up to the Givati Parking Lot and then underground to the Davidson Center inside the Old City. The pool is mentioned in the New Testament as the place where Jesus performed a miracle, so they're trying to attract more Christian visitors to the City of David. The City of David guides are now talking about how pilgrims washed themselves at the pool before walking up the trail and going to the Temple Mount/Haram al-Sharif inside the Old City. I wouldn't be surprised in a couple years to see people, dressed in what they think are clothes from Biblical times, re-enacting that ritual, going through the tunnel up to the Givati Parking Lot, and then underground to arrive at the Western Wall.

"The people in Silwan believe that construction of the Pilgrim's Trail is what's led to the new damage to houses on Wadi Hilweh Road. Unfortunately, we don't have the scientific evidence to prove it in court. A small nonprofit like ours can't afford the engineering tests, and neither can the residents of Silwan."

"I know that Emek Shaveh has worked hard to document how Elad and the Israeli Antiquities Authority are using archeology to take over Palestinian homes and to erase a lot of the history of the area," I said. "But the excavations keep happening. Do Israelis support your efforts? Do you feel hopeful?"

"Between the tunnels and the parks and the national monuments and the holy sites, [Israel has] created a web of nonnegotiable territory that's turning into all of East Jerusalem."

"If we manage through the courts to stall or delay construction that is harmful to the archeology or to the residents, then we see those as achievements. It's like a drop of water in the sea, but this is what we can do. As long as we have these small victories, we'll keep going.

"Unfortunately, to Israelis, the narrative of a united Jerusalem is very strong. It's hard for them to let go of the euphoria that came with conquering the Old City in 1967. Most Israelis say, 'We will never relinquish sovereignty over the Old City.'

"The success of the right-wing movement is that they are incorporating more and more Palestinian land into what Israelis consider the nonnegotiable territory of the Old City. The City of David is a perfect example of that. Between the tunnels and the parks and the national monuments and the holy sites, they've created a web of nonnegotiable territory that's turning into all of East Jerusalem."

As I walked back to Silwan, I thought over what Talya had said. I knew that most Israelis didn't think about Palestinians except as "terrorists," but I was depressed by our conversation. After learning about the impact of the 1967 war from a Palestinian perspective, to hear that Israelis were "euphoric" was horrifying.

Mired in my own thoughts, I got lost. I found myself on a long, dusty uphill road that didn't look at all familiar. There didn't seem to be anyone around. Finally I came upon a gray-bearded Palestinian man collecting aluminum cans at the side of the road. Luckily, he spoke excellent English, which he learned in school many years ago. We walked together until he needed to stop to rest. He told me that his family had lived in Jerusalem for 100 years, on Mt. Zion. He explained that he injured his shoulder some years ago and couldn't work at a regular job, although he had six children to feed. As we said good-bye, he gave me directions that took me back to Wadi Hilweh Street.

Odai Qareen with children at summer camp. (Credit: Madaa Creative Center)

30

"HOW COULD WE SUPPORT THE HUNGER STRIKE?":
ODAI'S STORY

The day before the *hafla*, Madaa's graduation party, Odai and I found time to talk. I wanted to know how he was doing and what was happening with the hip-hop group.

As Majd had told me, Odai was working part-time at Madaa, so we met up there. I never would have recognized him; he seemed so much older—clearly an adult.

"The last time we talked was two years ago," I said. "What's new?"

"My life has changed a lot, as a college student and as a rapper," he said.

"I remember you were going to be a business major. Is that still true?"

"No. I took some business classes, but I couldn't see myself being a businessman. Now my major is sociology. I see sociology as a way to help other people in our center, in our neighborhood, in our country."

"How is being at the university different from high school?"

"It is a whole different culture. Here in Palestine, our schools are separated by gender, so I always went to school just with other boys. But in the university, it's mixed. And the work is harder. But it's fun.

"And now I'm friends with students from all over the West Bank. I love how different hip-hop is in the different areas. I have

"There was nothing else I could do, so I wrote a song"

a friend from Jericho. We rap together in the festivals at the university. I'm meeting other rappers and we can do projects together, too."

"How is Dandara doing?"

"As we've gotten older, the group has gotten smaller. There are three of us left, and we are working on our second album."

"How has the music you're writing changed?"

"I'm drawing from a wider range of rappers: old school, swag, different types of rap. I've been listening to a lot of rap from Jordan lately. Salem Hadid really knows how to write his song; he is a smart guy. Chris Jobi is another Jordanian rapper I like. I'm listening to Shadi Loftram from Ramallah. And Project Chaos includes rappers from different parts of Palestine. One of them, Fadi Amous, was my teacher.

"Recently, I wrote a song about something that happened to my family and me. Settlers came into my uncle's house at four in the morning and they took it from us. They beat my father right in front of my eyes. That same night, they took twenty-four houses in the Wadi Hilweh neighborhood. They are still there today, with Israeli flags flying from my uncle's house. They beat me and kicked me out of my uncle's house. It was a terrible day. There was nothing else I could do, so I wrote a song:

> I awoke in the morning to my neighbors' screams.
> Suddenly I was in the street.
> Don't know who woke me up.
> The owners were not there,
> And the absentee properties guards were yelling.
> I was kicked outside my house, and they took away my place
> My words reach them
> Some sold, some got beaten, but my word kept going
> Suddenly, Israelis were my neighbors
> They changed the alphabets

They even changed the street name
They take oaths in His name, but how will they ever
escape their God?
Shame on them
This is your home
How can you sell it?
How can you recall your memories there?

"That's beautiful. I'm glad Dandara is still happening."

"And now there's a new group of young kids who have formed a hip-hop group at Madaa. The youngest is only seven years old. They are already writing and performing their own songs. I help them a little bit, but it's their words. It's good for them to say how they feel."

"Odai," I said, "I want to ask you about something else. Noura, one of the girls I interviewed, told me about the hunger strike of Palestinian political prisoners that's happening now. Majd told me there were support demonstrations in Silwan. What do students at the university think about the strike?"

"It's called the Dignity Strike. The prisoners' demands are about their human rights in prison.[48] At the university, we talked about how to support the strike. A group of us were chatting on Facebook about what we could do. We decided to go on a short hunger strike to show that we were with them.

"So I stopped eating, and just had water and salt for three days. It was last week, from Monday until Thursday. Even for that short time it was hard. May Allah help them.

"One of my friends from Silwan was arrested a year ago and

....
48   More than 1,500 Palestinian prisoners participated in the Dignity Strike, which began April 17, 2017. After forty days, the prisoners won a negotiated settlement, which included improved healthcare, increased family visits, and use of the canteen. For more information, see Addameer. "On Seventh Day: Mass Hunger Strike Continues Despite Escalation." 23 April 2017. 10 September 2020 <www.addameer.org/news/ seventh-day-mass-hunger-strike-continues-despite-escalation>.

sentenced to four years in prison. He is a part of the hunger strike. He's eighteen. I am proud of him. It's difficult because they have spent twenty-four days without food already."

"I hope they win their demands soon," I said, thinking about what prison was like for Nidal.

After a minute or two, I asked, "What are your plans after you finish your degree?"

"I want to get a master's degree in social science. Silwan is my home, my city. But for my master's degree, I might go to Europe. Maybe Spain.

"Then I want to return to Silwan to help our children learn early how to deal with the hardships of occupation. We want to give them the strength to continue to believe that we're the ones entitled to live here. We will remain standing on this land and teach, because education is the strongest weapon."

31
GRADUATION PARTY: THE HAFLA!

The next day was the hafla. People started coming to set up about eleven in the morning. We arranged sixty chairs on the deck in front of the apartment, leaving space for a small stage at the front.

We stacked boxes and boxes of muffins in plastic wrap and juice boxes in my room; after the performances it would be time for snacks. The front office was cleared out and became an exhibition space for the photography class.

The women from the crafts classes brought their work in for the show in their space. The intricacy of the embroidery was amazing—complicated geometric designs in red and white cross-stitch on black fabric; red and green on white fabric. Each woman who came kissed everyone else on both cheeks. There was so much warmth. Many of the women had brought food to share, and they spent lots of time deciding and redeciding the best way to arrange their work. We made tea and I brought out the last of my late-night chocolate stash.

Most of the staff at the center were young, but many of the women participating in the crafts classes were older. Most were dressed for the occasion in thawb with embroidered panels down the front and on the sleeves. It was sunny and very hot. I watched one woman in her long-sleeved, ankle-length black robe, her head covered with a black hijab, roll up the sleeves on her little boy's short-sleeved t-shirt so he wouldn't be too hot.

A gymnastics class performs at the hafla. (Credit: Madaa Creative Center)

As we were setting up, Majd and Odai helped the boys and girls in the new hip-hop group rehearse. Majd and Odai were endlessly patient and encouraging, and the kids worked for several hours before their performance. Lyf was seven years old. He's Nihad's son and the youngest member of the group. Majd told me that Lyf started memorizing all the Dandara songs when he was five, and now he was writing his own songs.

The hafla was scheduled to start at three. At three o'clock, almost no one was there, and then twenty minutes later almost 200 people, mostly young kids, were crammed into that small space. We put out more chairs, but many of the children ended up sitting on the ground in front, and many of the adults stood around the perimeter. Jawad, who had been out of the country, arrived in time to greet everyone and help hang dark plastic sheets over the deck to shield us from the hot sun.

The emcee was a girl of eleven or twelve; she did a great job of keeping the program moving and the enthusiasm high. No one made much of an effort to quiet the crowd down, so there were kids standing on chairs and people calling out to each other during the performances, but no one seemed to mind. Everyone was happy to be there and proud of the performers.

When the young hip-hop group performed, Odai stood up on a chair in the back, waving his arms in the air, clapping and singing along.

There were three debka dance groups, a choir, violinists, and two gymnastics groups that performed to drums. When the young hip-hop group performed, Odai stood up on a chair in the back, waving his arms in the air, clapping, singing along, filling the young performers with confidence.

Then the teachers awarded certificates to everyone who completed classes. When they got to the women's crafts workshops, they called up the women one by one. Everyone cheered; it was one of the most popular moments. Each woman came up, kissed her teacher on both cheeks, was photographed with the teacher and joined the others on stage. Then each class was photographed with their certificates.

Finally it was time to hand out the muffins and juice. In a matter of minutes, they were gone and the crowd started to thin out. Soon folks were loading the chairs into a truck and sweeping up the trash. The hafla was over and the deck was empty.

As Jawad got ready to leave, I told him how impressed I had been with the children's performances at the hafla, and with the community spirit that had pervaded the event.

Everyone here squeezed life into the cracks and crevices of the occupation.

"We try to give each child the feeling that they are important in society," Jawad said. "But we are very small. If you talk about Silwan alone, there are 25,000-30,000 children under the age of eighteen. So we need many centers, many Madaas."

"What do you think will happen, Jawad?" I asked. "How do you see the future for Silwan? For Palestine?"

"The Israeli occupation has not been smart in how it has dealt with the Palestinians. Ben Gurion [prime minister of Israel from 1948 to 1953, and from 1955 to 1963] said the old people will die and the young people will forget.

"When Ben Gurion said this, he thought: We don't have to invest in a Palestinian agreement, we don't have to convince them this is a good thing. They will just forget and this country will be ours. So Israel did not allow Palestinians to build, they did not allow us to move freely, they did not allow the refugees to return home.

"But it isn't happening that way. Ben Gurion was wrong. We have not forgotten.

"If you spoke with me twelve years ago, I would have told you: OK, Oslo is a tough agreement, but let's do it. Oslo didn't work. Today, we need a different solution. There are twelve million Palestinians all over the world. At least half of them have not given up. They want to return to their homeland. As Palestinians, according to all international agreements, we are under occupation and we have the right to struggle.[49]

"I don't want our children to throw stones. I want them to learn, to get an education, but look at our situation. My son has

....
49   UN Resolution 45/130 (December 14, 1990) "reaffirms the legitimacy of the struggle of peoples for independence, territorial integrity, national unity and liberation from colonial domination, apartheid and foreign occupation by all available means, including armed struggle."

been arrested two times; the first time he was six and half years old, the second time he was nine years old. They arrested him with a broken leg. So what can I tell him? Don't fight, don't struggle against this occupation? No, I will not tell him that. He has the right to struggle."

That night, my last night in Silwan, sitting on the quiet deck, I thought about my time there. I was so glad I got to see the hafla. I had heard many stories about the sense of community in Silwan, and about the impact of Madaa on people's lives. But it was different to see for myself how excited the children were to be together and to show their parents what they had learned; to see the community among the craftswomen, to feel the love and respect everyone had for the teachers and the Madaa staff. It filled me with hope.

I had learned so much about Silwan from the interviews and from watching how everyone here squeezed life into the cracks and crevices of the occupation: providing the children with as much love and support as possible, building resistance to the destruction of Silwan into every piece of their lives, holding on to Palestinian culture in every hip-hop performance, every meal, every embroidery stitch. The power of resilience: This was what I had to take home, what I wanted to share with youth and their families back in the United States.

PART IV

FREEDOM TO STAY, FREEDOM TO GO, FREEDOM TO RETURN

Lara Kiswani waiting to speak at a May Day demonstration in Oakland, CA, May 1, 2017.
(Credit: Brooke Anderson)

32
"THE RIGHT OF RETURN": LARA'S STORY

Back home, I needed to figure out how to finish this book. What was most important to emphasize? When I interviewed youth in Silwan, I always asked them what was most important to them, what they wanted to tell youth in the United States.

"Tell our story," they all said.

"Tell them how we live, and how difficult it is to live under the occupation with the constrictions that the Israelis put on us," Areen said.

"Tell them that we're always in fear they'll take someone away, our brother, our cousin, our uncle," said Dalal. "Or maybe our homes will be threatened, or we might get accused of something we didn't do and end up shot and dead."

"They should be careful when they're reading books or on social media," Bayan said. "When they read history books at school, they should notice who wrote it and whose story gets told. They should be careful about the media. Don't agree without thinking, without seeing. And tell them they're welcome to come to Palestine to see for themselves!"

"What else?" I asked.

"Tell them," many of the youth said, "that the United States should stop supporting Israel."

"Tell them," others said, "to be part of BDS!"

Their comments reminded me that, along with providing a space for Palestinian youth to tell their stories, I needed to share

"Tell them to be part of BDS!"

ways that we in the United States can be in solidarity with Palestine. From my own experience with Block the Boat, when we stopped Israel's ZIM shipping line from using the Port of Oakland, I knew how powerful the campaign to boycott, divest from, and sanction Israel could be.

I also knew that there is a huge debate about BDS in the United States. Zionists, often backed by money and direction from Israel, have campaigned to make it illegal to support BDS. They are panicked because the BDS movement has many supporters internationally and has had an important impact on supporting Palestinian rights. For example, Veolia, an international water, waste, and energy corporation, closed all operations in Israeli-occupied territory. They were responding to a worldwide BDS campaign that cost the firm an estimated $20 billion. A growing number of US churches—including the Episcopal, Presbyterian (USA), and United Methodist Churches, the United Church of Christ and the Quaker Friends—have divested from companies like Hewlett Packard, Caterpillar, and SodaStream over their role in Israeli violations of international law. So have the governments of Norway, Luxembourg, and New Zealand, and wealthy individuals like Bill Gates.

In 2005, when Palestinian organizations and unions called for the international campaign to boycott, divest from, and sanction Israel, they listed three demands:

- End the occupation and colonization of all Arab lands and dismantle the apartheid wall
- Recognize the fundamental right of Palestinians inside 1948 Israel to full equality
- Respect, protect, and promote the rights of Palestinian refugees to return to their homes and properties as stipulated in UN Resolution 194

UN Resolution 194, which was passed in December 1948, only a few months after Israel declared itself a Jewish state, says:

> Refugees wishing to return to their homes and live at peace
> with their neighbors should be permitted to do so at the earli-
> est practicable date, and that compensation should be paid for
> the property of those choosing not to return and for loss of or
> damage to property which, under principles of international
> law or equity, should be made good by the Governments or
> authorities responsible.[50]

I knew how important it was to Yacoub to be able to return to Lifta, and how important it was for the Palestinians in Silwan to be able to stay in their homes. But I wondered how Palestinians in the diaspora—those who had been forced out of their homes and out of their country in 1948 or 1967—felt about the right of return now. Especially two or three generations later. I decided to ask.

I was already friends with folks at the Arab Resource and Organizing Center, so I headed across the Bay to talk with them. AROC's office is on the second floor of a walk-up in San Francisco's Mission District, through two doors and up a narrow set of stairs. Their office is one crowded room, filled with staff and visitors, and a small separate space where lawyers help people with immigration problems. Despite phones ringing and overlapping conversations in English and Arabic, everyone jumps up to hug you when you walk in.

Lara Kiswani, AROC's busy executive director, made time to talk to me. Like everyone I talked to in Silwan, she started with her family history in Palestine:

"My mother's family is from Acre, which is in 1948 Palestine. My mother's village was ethnically cleansed[51] in 1948. They were

....

50   United Nations General Assembly. The Question of Palestine. 10 September 2020 <www.un.org/unispal/data-collection/general-assembly>.

51   The UN Commission of Experts defines ethnic cleansing as "a purposeful policy designed by one ethnic or religious group to remove by violent and terror-inspiring means the civilian population of another ethnic or religious group from certain geographic areas."

> **"Indigenous people maintaining their ceremonies and their cultures ... gave me so much inspiration, like they were saying to me, 'We're still fighting, we still have hope. So you should, too.'"**

forced to leave by foot and ended up in Gaza, in the city of Rafah. The family was split up, and eventually my grandmother ended up in Jordan. So my mother was born as a refugee in Jordan.

"My father was born in Beit Iksa, in the district of Jerusalem. His family fled Beit Iksa in 1948 when they heard about the Deir Yassin massacre, which was very close by. They assumed the same was going to happen to them if they stayed. There were thirteen children in the family. In the chaos of fleeing the village, they forgot the baby, who was less than a year old. My grandmother assumed somebody else was carrying her. They were miles away before they counted the children and realized one of the daughters was missing. Frantic, they sent a few folks back to find her, and there she was, sitting alone in the house, crying. So that was the story my aunt grew up hearing: how she was saved from the hands of the Israeli military, but also that she was abandoned. And we, the next generation, grew up learning that story, too.

"After the state of Israel was created and the worst of the Nakba massacres ended, my father's family returned to Beit Iksa, which was under Jordanian control. Many of the houses had been destroyed, but the village was able to survive, at least for a few years. During the 1967 war, Beit Iksa was occupied by Israel and my father's family was forced to move to Jordan.

"During my father's first marriage, he lived in Jordan, and my older siblings were born there. I am the first in my family to be born in the United States.

"Growing up Palestinian in the United States politicized me in a particular way. I went to Arabic school every week. Most of the students at the school were Palestinian, so we learned Palestinian songs, Palestinian history, and how to read and write our own language. I was always excited to go to Arabic school. I felt at home, like I belonged. I felt connected in ways I never felt in regular school. There wasn't one other Arab person, let alone a Palestinian, in my elementary school. Most of the kids were white, but there was a mix of students of color, and we all circled up together.

"One day when I was in the second grade, all the kids were supposed to go up to the map and point to where their ancestors were from. I remember everyone pointing to the map, mostly Europe, but also Mexico, the Philippines, maybe Vietnam or Korea. When it was my turn, I went to point to Palestine, but of course it wasn't marked on the map. So I pointed to the area labeled 'Israel' and said, 'I'm from here: Palestine.'

"The teacher said, 'That doesn't exist.'

"I said, 'Oh, yes, it does. I know where I'm from.'

"I grew up with my grandma—my mother's mother—and her stories about Acre. When she was young, living in Acre, her neighbor was Jewish and it was never a problem. Then, in 1948, the Nakba happened. Suddenly that Jewish neighbor was the only one allowed to stay, and my grandmother's family had to leave. My grandma's stories about Palestine were the most vivid because she held onto the images and the smells. I felt like I was there with her.

"So I felt confident challenging my teacher. Even in second grade, I understood that part of being Palestinian is challenging authority. I knew if I didn't stand up for myself and assert my existence, I would be invisible. People would deny that my family's history even occurred."

"Aside from that second-grade teacher," I asked, "did you face discrimination at school for being Palestinian or for being Muslim?"

> **"I knew if I didn't stand up for myself and assert my existence, I would be invisible. People would deny that my family's history even occurred."**

"When I was in fourth grade, I thought I was doing everything right, like the other kids in my circle of friends, but I couldn't raise my grade above a B. 'Why am I the only one getting a B?' I'd wonder.

"Then the first Gulf War against Iraq began in 1990, and we had to write letters to soldiers. The way that teacher described Iraqi people, all Arabs, was in stereotypes. 'They don't even use forks and spoons.' she said.

"'That's not true!' I argued. 'Some meals we don't eat with forks and spoons, but most we do.' I constantly challenged this teacher in front of all my classmates, but I never understood what was happening.

"When I got to fifth grade, I had a teacher who treated me like everyone else. That was the strangest feeling. Suddenly I was getting straight A's and thriving in school. And then, in sixth grade, I had the best teacher. She was Filipina; she had taught my siblings and she knew my family. She invited me to help her teach Islamic studies. She and I co-taught it to the class. That was when I realized how it feels to be respected as a young person.

"In middle school, I joined MEChA.[52] There was no Palestinian club or Arab club, so MEChA was the political club. It was a way to be engaged civically and to be connected to a political community.

"Then, while I was at the University of California-Davis, the Second Intifada broke out in 2000. I was already part of starting an Arab organization there, and we decided we needed to support the uprising. So, together with students at UC-Berkeley, we started Students for Justice in Palestine. That's how I became a full-time activist."

"Why is the right of return such a big deal?" I asked Lara. "Is it important to you?"

"My mother wasn't able to visit Palestine until she had an American passport, when I was already an adult. My grandmother,

....

52   MEChA is a Chicanx student movement organization. The acronym, in Spanish, stands for *Movimiento Estudiantil Chicano/a de Aztlan.*

who was forced to leave in 1948, died without ever being able to return. The fact that my family couldn't go back to Palestine until we had US passports is really disgusting. That's the reality for most Palestinian Americans. When you finally get to go, you're coming to Palestine, to your own village, not as a Palestinian, but as an American.

"So the right of return means that all of us, no matter what generation we are, have the right to choose to go back to our original homelands to live, to visit, to cultivate the land there. And that choice is a right for all Palestinian refugees, all 7.5 million of us.

"The right of return means that all of us, no matter what generation we are, have the right to choose to go back to our original homelands to live, to visit, to cultivate the land there."

"There are more Palestinians living outside of Palestine than inside. Many of us still carry the keys to our original homes. The United Nations has been saying since 1948 that we have the right to return, but Israel has never allowed that to happen.

"If Palestinians living generation after generation in refugee camps in Lebanon, in Syria, in Jordan—if they don't all have the choice to go home and participate in the future of Palestine, then we're not talking about a free Palestine—we're just talking about the fraction of the population that was lucky enough to be able to stay in the country. That's not justice or liberation.

"These are issues that everyone's talking about now: people's freedom to move, to stay, to return. People should have the freedom to be wherever they want or need to be. And those who have been forced out have a right to return. That's a fundamental human right.

"That's why it's one of the three BDS demands."

"I have one more question," I said. "How do you see Palestine connected to other issues in the United States?"

"One of the most moving things for me growing up was when

I finally learned about the Indigenous history of this country. In school I learned something about the horrors of slavery and I felt connected to Black students because of a shared, yet different, experience of oppression. But slavery was treated in the classroom like it was something in the distant past, with no implications for now. And we never really talked about Native American history. It wasn't until I was older that I realized: Oh wait, the United States was also built on colonial conquest and the ethnic cleansing of an Indigenous population. We're not the first people to experience this.

"That blew my mind. I realized that Palestine isn't an exception. It's never good for us to think our experiences are exceptional. It made me feel more connected to a universal humanity. I started to understand myself differently: Oh, that's how being Palestinian fits into the world. And the reverse is true, too. I think it's helpful for other communities of color to understand Palestine.

"Every year there's a sunrise ceremony at Alcatraz Island to celebrate Indigenous Peoples' Thanksgiving.[53] The first time I went, I thought: I don't want that to be us—people who have lost so much land that people gather every year in some city in Palestine to honor our history. And we share a ceremony with these 'supporters,' who then leave and forget about it for the rest of the year.

"And then I realized: Wow, after so many years, here are Indigenous people maintaining their ceremonies and their cultures. Every year they're here. Every day they're still honoring their history and their indigeneity on this land. That gave me so much inspiration, like they were saying to me, 'We're still fighting, we still have hope. So you should, too.'

"That experience made me committed to my struggle in ways

....

53   Indigenous Peoples' Thanksgiving is a commemoration of the nineteen-month occupation of Alcatraz Island in San Francisco Bay by Native American activists from 1969-1971.

that hadn't happened before. It gave me a spark of hope and an understanding of what I want to fight for and against, lessons I wanted to learn from our Indigenous counterparts.

"Another year, a group of us Palestinians were invited to do debka as part of the ceremony at Alcatraz. Dancing there as the sun came up, I said to myself: Yes, this is the world I want to fight for!"

33
"I FELT LIKE I WAS HOME": AYESHA'S STORY

Lara had to get back to work, but she arranged for me to inter-view Ayesha, a Palestinian teenager living in San Francisco. Ayesha had been a member of AROC's Arab Youth Organization since ninth grade. She had just graduated from high school in San Francisco, and was about to start her first year at a California state university. I asked her if she had visited Palestine.

"I've been to Palestine twice. The first time was in 2012, when I was ten years old.

"Palestine was beautiful. I felt like I was home. Don't get me wrong: San Francisco is my home, but Palestine is my actual home. I felt like I belonged.

"But I also felt like I didn't belong, because every mile or less you have to go through another Israeli checkpoint. You have to have your visa on you all the time. Even as a little kid with my US passport, they questioned everything I did and everywhere I went. Even now, I don't want you to say what university I'm going to because I'm afraid this interview could mean they won't let me into Palestine next time.

"On that trip, first we spent a few days in Beit Hanina, my mom's village, which is near Jerusalem. Lots of people speak English there. Even though Israel's 2012 assault on Gaza[54] was

....

54   In November 2012, Israel launched an eight-day aerial attack on Gaza. One hundred and seventy-four Palestinians and six Israelis died as a result of Operation Pillar Defense.

happening while we were there, we could go out on the street and go visit people. It was fun.

"My dad is from a smaller village near Bethlehem and it's much tenser there because there's an Israeli settlement right across the street. It wasn't safe to even go outside. Just to get to my grandpa's land, where he grew vegetables and stuff, we had to go through an Israeli checkpoint.

"My grandpa was excited to show us what he was growing: tomatoes, cucumbers, all kinds of vegetables. That's really 'farm to table.' They pick vegetables that they grow on their land and that's what is for dinner. Not like here where we buy everything at the store. My grandpa had so much joy on his face when he talked about his land.

"The next time I went was in 2015, when there were many clashes in Jerusalem. Even in Beit Hanina, we weren't allowed to go outside. On both trips, I learned a lot of Arabic, but I still understood more than I could speak. It was confusing, being Palestinian and not being fluent in Arabic. There were times when I felt like 'this is my home, but I can't fully connect because I grew up in America speaking English, not here, speaking Arabic.'"

"What does the right to return mean to you?" I asked.

"It means going back without being interrogated. It means I can go anywhere I want without guns being pointed at me. It means no walls, no borders, no checkpoints. And for me as a Palestinian who's grown up in the United States, it means I can go home to Palestine feeling safe, not like I have a target on my back."

"What issues have you faced in school as a Palestinian?"

"It's a struggle. I don't feel represented. I've been in the [San Francisco] school district for twelve years, and we've never studied anything about Arab history, Arab Americans in the United States, or about Palestine.

"And then there are the ignorant comments. When you're the one being targeted, it's hard to even comprehend what's happening. It's like: 'Are you serious? You're speaking like that about me, about my people, right in front of me?'

"In my pre-law class, the teacher announced that the topic for one of our class debates was: Should the United States stop funding Israel? I was surprised he even brought it up. But then the students in my class said things like 'the Palestinians deserve it,' 'they're terrorists,' 'so what, it's not their land anyway.' And the teacher just let those comments go through.

"It was painful sitting there. And how do I even respond? If I try to speak up, maybe they'll think: What does she know? She might be Palestinian, but Palestine doesn't exist.

"I was afraid to talk to the teacher because he said he had family from Israel. He told the class he didn't agree with Israel, but if he was truly an ally, he would have stopped those comments.

"If I started talking, I might not be able to stop, and I might end up in trouble. I truly wanted to pass his class and I just didn't know which way he was leaning. It's hard when you have your grade on the line."

"What would have made things easier at school?"

"It would have made such a difference if our history was taught, if we were in the curriculum. And hard as that would be, if the truth was taught.

"When we fill out forms for our school, having a simple little box to check would make it so much better. I'm tired of being 'other' all the time. In elementary school, I'd make my own box and I'd label it Arab or Palestinian. Having to check 'other' makes you feel like you don't belong and you're not part of anybody.

"With all the languages they teach in San Francisco schools, they just started to teach Arabic. I wish I could go back in time and be a little kid right now so I could take Arabic in elementary school. I'm glad that it's not too late for everybody else.

"Another thing that would help is more Arab teachers. My junior year, I actually had a Palestinian teacher and that was so important to me, especially because she was a Palestinian

"Being an ally, that's the first step to being amazing."

woman. I connected with her so much, and I actually felt secure in her class. I felt much more strongly unapologetic about being Palestinian.

"And finally, every ally builds us up a little bit stronger. So I hope kids who read this book get educated, speak up, and help us get curriculum in our schools about Palestinians, Arabs, and other folks who are ignored. The more allies we have, the louder our cause is and the more united we are.

"Being an ally, that's the first step to being amazing."

34
PALESTINE IN OUR HEARTS

As I was thanking Ayesha and packing up my stuff, Lara darted back in the room. "There's something I forgot to tell you," she said. "It's five years since we blocked the ZIM ship, and we're thinking of having a party to celebrate the anniversary. What do you think?"

"That's a great idea," I said. "What can I do to help?"

"Can you do the food?"

About a month later, we had the celebration on a Saturday night at the storefront next to AROC's office. As folks gathered, there was Palestinian music in the background, and a video of the

Arab American youth leading a march to block Israel's ZIM ship in Oakland, CA, October 20, 2014. (Credit: Jackie Brown)

Block the Boat march played against one wall. I set up the food in the back. So many people came, we soon spilled out the door and onto the sidewalk. Once we had a critical mass, we closed the street at both ends, and the whole celebration moved to the middle of the street. A Korean drumming group played while debka dancers made a big circle surrounded by the clapping, cheering crowd. Then we went back inside to eat, visit, and talk with friends we hadn't seen for a long time.

During our party, I kept flashing back to the hafla in Silwan. It was a reminder of how important it is to keep Palestine in our hearts and minds, to act in solidarity—and to have joyous celebrations along the way.

(Credit: Art Forces)

AFTERWORD

February 1, 2021

I returned to Silwan in June 2019, co-leading a group of teachers who were learning first-hand about Palestine so they could teach it in their classrooms. We spent a wonderful morning in Silwan, but I didn't have a chance to talk one-on-one with folks at Madaa. So just before *Determined to Stay* when to press, I called Sahar to catch up. Of course, the impact of the pandemic was on the top of our minds.

"How has the coronavirus affected Silwan?" I asked her.

"To be honest," Sahar said, "for us as Palestinians, in the beginning it wasn't clear what was happening. Here, there were only rumors. You have to remember: For decades the information we have received from the Israeli Municipality has been lies directed at forcing us out of our homes, so it's hard to believe anything they say. We were suddenly told that schools were closed and we were not to go more than 100 meters from our houses, but we didn't get any information about why. So in the beginning, many of us thought, 'It's another conspiracy.'

"By April 2020, we started to see Covid cases here, and we saw how dangerous it was. When everything closed down, the settlers got services, but we didn't. Our women's committee was active from the beginning, helping people who needed food or who needed money. But when we organized to help each other, many people were arrested: Palestinians cleaning the plaza in front of al-Aqsa were arrested, medical workers who established a testing

"At first, we were in shock …What should we do?"

site in Silwan were arrested, people trying to distribute food packages were arrested. Giving a basket of food to a poor family—what harm could that do?

"This is one more crisis we have on top of the occupation. The Israelis use every emergency to make things worse for us. So, during the lockdowns, the streets in Silwan and the Old City are filled with police. They don't bother the settlers, but if a Palestinian child doesn't have their mask on just right, they get arrested and the fines are very expensive. This is a child: just show them how to do it! If a Palestinian shop opens, the fine for the shopkeeper can equal a year's worth of income. Meanwhile, the City of David's excavations go on without stopping. The house demolitions continue. The municipality recently issued eviction orders that will make 120 people homeless—in the middle of a pandemic.

"For the children here in Silwan, like children all over the world, it's a big problem that the schools have been closed. I am afraid that they have gained nothing this year. On a psychosocial level, if we had problems before, now it's much worse. The children have lost their connection with school, with learning. I am just waiting until we can be with them again.

"If a teacher has thirty students in a class, sometimes only two or three will be there online. In general, the children are using phones, but it's not easy. If you have many children in the house, one phone or one computer is not enough.

"Access to the internet is even more of a problem. In the beginning, we received many donations, so families got internet access for one or two months, but then the money ran out. I'm following one family to see how their young boy is doing after being arrested and imprisoned. His mom told me, 'I have five kids, but I only have one phone and we don't have internet access, so they aren't going to school at all.'

"I told her, 'When Madaa is open, we have computers here,

please send your kids to the center.' She told me, 'I am worried about the settlers and the police. It's a dangerous route from our house to the center. I'm afraid they will be arrested or killed. I prefer them illiterate but not arrested.' She is saying this in sorrow, but it is the reality."

"How has Madaa tried to support children and their families during the pandemic?"

"At first, we were in shock. All the schools were closed. What should we do? In the beginning, our decision was to keep the centers running so the children would have someplace to go. We were the last institution in Silwan to close our doors. When we were forced to close, we had many meetings to figure out how to change our services. In these difficult times, it doesn't make sense to separate from your community. They need you more than ever. At this point, we're on our fourth lockdown. By now, we know how to plan, we have a program for every week. Time gives you experience, teaches you how to adjust to the situation.

"Of course, we are building on how strong the Madaa Creative Center has grown in the past few years. Before the pandemic, we were having winter camp as well as summer camp. We added a film series. We had a class for women activists to teach them how to use their cameras to document human rights abuses. We had a workshop for teenagers on their rights. We took the children on a trip to the Negev where they got to ride camels!

"The question was: how to adapt? Our priority was providing psychosocial support to children and families. So we made video clips of art activities that children can do with materials available in their homes. We showed them how to make play dough and they sent us pictures and videos of their projects. For Palestinian Land Day, we uploaded a video with projects recycling plastic bottles. The children shared pictures of their projects and videos of themselves singing. We use chat groups to support their school work.

"For women, we sent how-to videos and audio recordings for skills like embroidery, sewing, and making natural soaps. We use chat groups to help parents deal with the stress the pandemic is creating for children and families. Our mental health department continues its weekly meetings with teenagers, except now the meetings are online."

"What amazing work," I said. "This has been such a hard year. Right now, what's giving you hope for the future of Silwan?"

"What gives me hope is believing in our children, believing in the next generation. They deserve to have their future. This is what keeps us fighting."

ACKNOWLEDGMENTS

I am honored and grateful to have had the opportunity to spend time with a small piece of the Silwani community. I can never sufficiently express my gratitude to Jawad Siyam, Sahar Abbasi, Majd Ghaith, and Bayan Abassi. Despite overwhelming workloads and constant crises, the staff of Madaa Creative Center and Wadi Hilweh Information Center spent hours talking to me, setting up interviews, translating, finding photos, reviewing the manuscript, and supporting this project in myriad ways. I especially want to thank the youth and members of the community who opened up their homes and their hearts to talk with me about their lives.

None of this would have been possible without Zeiad Abbas Shamrouch and the Middle East Children's Alliance (MECA). Zeiad, MECA's Executive Director, took on educating me about Palestine when I was a teacher with the right instincts but huge gaps in my understanding. He urged me to visit Palestine, where MECA's resources and contacts enabled my family and me to have a life-changing experience. Josie Shields Stromsness, MECA's Program Director, introduced us to Silwan during that first trip, and has put endless hours into supporting every visit I've made since. She's also been my go-to person for an endless stream of questions. MECA Finance Director Nancy Ippolito ensured that I had the resources and time to complete this project, and was instrumental in getting it published. The incredible printmaker and muralist Jos Sances created the beautiful cover image. A huge thank you to everyone on the MECA staff for their support.

Thanks to Nick Estes for the wonderful introduction. And to Ayesha, Corrina Gould, Talya Ezrahi, Lara Kiswani, and Zakaria and Yacoub Odeh for sharing their time, wisdom and stories with me.

As a writer, I want to acknowledge Margaret Randall as an extraordinary oral historian, revolutionary theorist, poet, and friend. Her books on the women of the Cuban and Nicaraguan revolutions have long been models for me as a political thinker and author, and I reread them often as I struggled with writing this book. When I decided that I couldn't write it after all, Margaret told me in no uncertain terms to get over myself and finish it. Then she read an early draft and gave me the encouragement I needed to start the next draft.

The maps in this book are the result of months of work by a long-time and wonderful friend, Henry (Camo) Bortman. Camo read an early draft of Determined to Stay, recklessly volunteered to help with the graphics, and became a partner in finishing this project. He essentially taught himself mapmaking to adapt maps from many sources to help explain the story of Silwan, and then spent hours with me over Zoom analyzing the political implications of every decision we made. Camo and I want to thank Jessica Andersen of Visualizing Palestine for maps documenting Israeli colonization of Palestine and permission to modify them, and for a high-resolution aerial image of Jerusalem's Old City and Silwan; Zoltán Grossman, Geography/Native American & Indigenous Studies at Evergreen State College, for useful sources of information about US colonization of Indigenous North American lands, and for poring over our maps with a fine-tooth comb; Passia, for Jan de Jong's map of Jerusalem's Old City and Silwan; Emek Shaveh, for permission to modify Lori Cohen's map of archeological sites in Silwan; and J. Bruce Jones, for permission to use the outline of the continental United States from his World Regional Maps Coloring Book.

Madaa generously shared their photography archive with me; thanks to Fidaa and Haneen for their work finding photographs, and then searching for high resolution versions. Thanks to Art Forces and the other photographers represented in this book for their beautiful work.

As a non-Arabic speaker, I relied on the help of wonderful translators in Silwan. On Ericka's and my trip, Nihad Siyam proved not only an excellent translator, but a source of invaluable background information. Bayan's enthusiasm for the project enabled many interviews that wouldn't have happened otherwise; her empathy and grace enriched many conversations. Sahar and Majd made time in their impossible schedules to facilitate and translate critical conversations. Afterwards, Anas Issa transcribed the Arabic interviews; Haneen Shahin and Dina Abdou the translations from Arabic to English. Eliana Rubin and Sherry Segers helped with English transcription. Patrick O'Neill, MECA's Bookkeeper and Administrative Coordinator, created consistency for the Arabic transliterations.

I was lucky to have friends and colleagues who were willing to read draft after draft of *Determined to Stay* and provide equal measures of encouragement and critique. Thanks to Mickey Ellinger, Henry Bortman, Margaret Randall, Zeiad Abbas Shamrouch, and Nancy Ippolito. Special thanks to Linda Ellman, who brought the eye of a history teacher and the heart of loving friend, and Samia Shoman, who contributed the perspective of a Palestinian educator. Cristina Salat provided helpful developmental editing suggestions.

Judy Rohrer invited me to use her Spokane apartment as a retreat when I needed a quiet space to write the final draft of this book. It was the perfect gift at the perfect time.

Zeiad and I have been facilitating workshops on teaching Palestine for more than a decade. Our discussions with teachers and activists across the country have played a major role in my growing understanding of the connections between the continuing colonial conquest in Palestine and in the United States. I am particularly indebted to Palestinian and other Arab educators and students, and to Indigenous educators and activists.

I have had the privilege of participating in the Palestine solidarity movement in the San Francisco Bay Area for many years. That movement, and particularly the leadership of the Arab Resource and Organizing Center, has been a continual source of support and growth.

Many thanks to Michel Moushabeck, Pam Fontes-May, and everyone at Interlink for bringing *Determined to Stay* to life.

And the deepest gratitude, of course, for my immediate family, Karen Shain and Ericka Sokolower-Shain. Karen and Ericka were part of my first trip to Palestine; Ericka was my partner for my second trip. Both read and reread drafts of the book, talked me through or down from innumerable crises along the way, and were unrelentingly supportive and encouraging. It's not easy to live with someone in the throes of writer's block. I love you both more than I can say.

GLOSSARY

Arabic	English
abu	Father
afwan	You're welcome
ahlan	Welcome
al-Aqsa Mosque	The third holiest site in Islam, located in the Old City in Jerusalem
al-Nakba	The catastrophe (refers to the 1948 violent expulsion of Palestinians from their homes and land by the Zionists)
al-Naksa	The setback (refers to the 1967 war in which Israel conquered the West Bank, including East Jerusalem, and Gaza)
adhan	Islamic call to prayer
bismillah	In the name of Allah. In Islam, saying *bismillah* brings blessings to the beginning of an activity.
debka	Traditional Palestinian folkloric dance
hafla	Party, celebration
hijab	Headscarf often worn by Muslim women outside the home
intifada	Uprising or rebellion
ka'ak	Sesame-seed covered bread that's baked in a ring or handbag shape

labna	Yogurt strained until it is thick and spreadable
maqluba	Literally, "upside down." Traditional Palestinian dish cooked in a large pot with layers of meat, potatoes, eggplant or other vegetables, and rice. When it is done, it is turned upside down onto a serving platter.
marhaba	Hi or hello
Ramadan	Ninth month of the Islamic calendar, observed by Muslims worldwide as a month of fasting, prayer, reflection, and community
thawb	Ankle-length dress or robe with long sleeves
um	Mother

Other Terms

absentee property laws	Israel's absentee property laws were originally written to legitimize Israelis moving into the homes of Palestinians forced out in 1948. More recently, they are being used to legitimize the theft by Israeli settlers of Palestinian homes and lands in East Jerusalem.
BDS	The Movement to Boycott, Divest from and Sanction Israel (BDS) started in 1995, when 170 Palestinian organizations and groups called on the international community to support Palestinian human rights by putting pressure on Israel. They were inspired by the international movement to boycott and divest from South Africa, an important piece of bringing down the apartheid government there in 1994.

| Oslo Accords | A set of agreements, signed September 13, 1993, between Israel and the Palestine Liberation Organization. Although the stated goal was a peaceful transition to two states, Palestine was chopped into further pieces and Israel maintained control of external security, resources, and borders. There was no resolution to Israel's continuing theft of Palestinian land, to Israel's illegal settlements in the West Bank, to the status of Jerusalem, or to the Palestinian right of return. |